Can I Hold Him?

Christmas Stories for All Ages

May these stories be a favourite part of your Advent preparations. Blessings! Rev. Janet Stobie

Written and Illustrated by
Janet Stobie

ISBN 978-0-9737986-1-6
Publisher: Child's Play Productions, Peterborough, Ontario K9H 7T1
www.janetstobie.com   *info@janetstobie.com*

DEDICATION

This book is dedicated to my husband Tom who has loved me through hours spent on the computer and who has shared his gift of editing.

ACKNOWLEDGMENTS

Without the people of Dunsford, Bethany, and Pontypool congregations, who listened to my stories on Sunday mornings, and encouraged me to publish them, I would never have started on this writer's journey. I am truly grateful for all of them.

I need also to thank my long-time friend, Nancy Miller, who has helped edit this book for both printings, and has listened to countless hours of book talk.

Without the patience, knowledge and perseverance of Greg Phillips, of Four Hundred and Four Business Solutions, I might never have overcome the technical problems of internet publishing.

Of course, there is my wonderful Tom, who not only shared his gifts of editing, but also brought me endless cups of tea and cheerfully encourages me to ignore him for hours at a time while I write.

CONTENTS

FOREWORD

Traditionally, we share our faith through the telling and retelling of stories. When we hear how God has acted in the lives of others today and down through the centuries, we come to understand how God acts in our lives.

The story of Jesus' birth is a favorite. Every year on Christmas Eve around the world, church communities gather to hear the ancient Christmas Story told once again. The nativity scene, showing Mary and Joseph with Jesus lying in the manger, is a common picture. Everywhere the story is told, the characters are portrayed as people of the local culture, but the story remains the same.

We think we know the stories well, and yet each year we come to them, hoping they will speak to us anew of God's love. As you read the stories in *Can I Hold Him?*, I ask you to let go of your preconceived ideas and hear the stories as if for the first time. For a few moments become Mary or Joseph or a young shepherd. Hear, see and feel through their hearts.

Read one story. Savor it. Think about it. Take the time needed to receive God's message of love for you.

ISN'T HE BEAUTIFUL!

The Birth of Jesus
Luke 2: 1-7 (NIV)

"In those days Caesar Augustus issued a decree that a census should be taken of the entire Roman world. 2 (This was the first census that took place while[a] Quirinius was governor of Syria.) 3 And everyone went to their own town to register.

4 So Joseph also went up from the town of Nazareth in Galilee to Judea, to Bethlehem the town of David, because he belonged to the house and line of David. 5 He went there to register with Mary, who was pledged to be married to him and was expecting a child. 6 While they were there, the time came for the baby to be born, 7 and she gave birth to her firstborn, a son. She wrapped him in cloths and placed him in a manger, because there was no guest room available for them."

Introduction:

In the middle of most pictures of the Christmas story sits a young woman, either holding the baby Jesus or looking down at him lying in the manger. She is often dressed in blue and almost always smiling. Her name is Mary. When Jesus was born, his mother was probably a young teenager, possibly fifteen, yet in her culture, she was already a woman. This is her story.

ISN'T HE BEAUTIFUL!
Mary's Story

One night, nine months ago, I was sitting at the window, dreaming about my wedding, when I heard a soft swish swishshshsh behind me. I whirled around. Over by the wall, in a circle of glowing light, stood an angel whose snow-white wings and robe gleamed in the candle light. Terrified, I grabbed my stool for protection.

"Don't be afraid," he said, "My name is Gabriel. You have been chosen by God to be the mother of a very special baby, who will be even greater than King David."

Amazed, I asked, "How can this be? I'm not even married yet?"

3

He smiled. His robe and face gleamed even brighter. "All things are possible with God," he assured me. "God's Spirit will come upon you, and you will give birth to a son and name him Jesus. This baby will be the long awaited Messiah, the Saviour, God's gift of love to the world." (NIV)

All young Jewish girls dream about being the mother of the Messiah. I felt honoured. Carefully, I set the stool down and took a step forward. Taking a deep breath for courage, I closed my eyes and made the glorious commitment, "Yes, I will follow God's will. I accept this holy task."

Gabriel nodded and faded from my sight.

All night I tossed and turned, too excited to sleep. When the sun finally rose above the horizon, I picked up the water bucket and raced to the well. On the way home, I stopped at Joseph's carpentry shop. "Joseph, Joseph," I called, swinging the bucket as I rushed through the door. Water slopped on the floor. I bent over and mopped it up with the bottom of my skirt. Joseph strode in from the back room, wiping his hands on his apron.

"This is a delightful surprise," he said, his pleasure showing on his face.

I straightened up and blurted out my news, "Joseph, I'm going to have a baby…"

"You're with child?" he interrupted and frowned. "Who did this to you, Mary?"

I reached out and gripped his arms, "An angel named Gabriel visited me last night. He said this baby was to be the promised Messiah, the Saviour of our people."

Joseph's frown deepened. He clenched his fists. "You can't be with child. We've never…" he stopped and then started again. "An angel? Why would God choose you…us? We're not rich." He shook his head. "The Messiah…No, no, no, no We're just ordinary people. We're not even married yet. No, it can't be…"

Shocked with his reaction, my joy disappeared. I started to cry.

Joseph reached out and wiped a tear from my cheek. He looked so sad. "Go home, Mary. Just go home."

I felt sick. What had happened? We were supposed to be happy…His hands shook as he held my bucket out to me. Silently, I left the shop, my mind filled with turmoil. My wonderful Joseph doesn't believe me, I thought. I did my chores as I wrestled with my thoughts. What will I do? To

5

be mother of the Messiah, I need Joseph. In my culture a woman without a husband is nothing. I will be an outcast. The day dragged into night. I sat at the window in my room and cried. I couldn't tell my mother. She might have the same reaction as Joseph. Once again, the night hours were endless.

The next morning Joseph came to our house, his face serious; he spoke with such intensity. "The angel Gabriel spoke to me in a dream, last night." His eyes filled with tears, "I'm sorry I didn't believe you, Mary."

Relief and joy filled my soul. Within a month we were married. I'm sure people wondered what was happening, but they said nothing. It was only when it became obvious that I was with child that the whispers started. Soon, our friends stopped speaking to us. Children in the street called me names and threw sticks and stones at me. No one believed about the angel.

"You're just ordinary people," they said. "Joseph is a carpenter. God wouldn't choose you to be the parents of the Messiah," They refused to understand. Have you ever been judged and found guilty by people who didn't know the whole story? It hurts terribly. Finally, I couldn't take their meanness any more. Joseph took me to visit my Aunt Elizabeth in another town. I knew I could trust her love for me.

Tearfully, I described my plight to her. She listened, tears running down her cheeks. She gave me a warm hug and rubbed my back.

"My friends laugh and criticize me too," she said. "They think I'm much too old to be with child...and I am. Zechariah and I prayed for a child for such a long time. After many years, one of God's angels appeared at the temple and announced to Zechariah that I would have a baby. Zechariah hasn't spoken since. Being with child is difficult when you're old. I get so tired."

Together, we shared our joy in our babies growing inside us. Aunt Elizabeth was God's blessing for me. I stayed with her as long as I could. When my time was near, Joseph came for me. I wanted to be home when our baby was born.

Three days after my return to Nazareth, a Roman soldier rode into town carrying a trumpet and a scroll. "Caesar Augustus has decreed that all the Roman world will be taxed," he announced. "You must return to the place of your birth to be registered for the census."

My Joseph was born in Bethlehem, one hundred miles from our home in Nazareth. I begged Joseph to take me with him. He understood. His friends taunted him with mean and cruel words, too. He wanted me to come, but he was worried about the journey. I was determined. Finally, he agreed to take me.

For safety, we joined a group of other travelers going to Bethlehem. Many of them were angry that they had to make the trip. They didn't offer friendship. I guess we didn't either. A cold rain fell on us every day. My back ached. I wanted to be with Joseph, but the journey went on and on. I thought it would never end. I kept telling myself to be thankful that I got to ride on the donkey. Joseph walked the whole way.

When we reached Bethlehem, none of our relatives would open their homes to us. We should have known our reputation would precede us. Most of them wouldn't even answer the door when we knocked. Those who did looked down their noses in disapproval and just shook their heads. Uncle Uzziah slammed the door in our faces.

"Joseph," I pleaded. "We have to find something. My labour has started."

The inn was our last resort. Joseph pounded on the door. A young servant girl answered.

"No room at this inn," she shouted without even looking at us. She tried to slam the door, but Joseph put his foot in the way.

"Go get your master," he demanded.

She scurried away. The smell of sweat and smoke oozed out the open door. Music, laughter, loud voices echoed through the walls. I didn't want to go in there, but where else could we go? Finally, the innkeeper came. Joseph tried to explain.

The innkeeper cut him off. "We're full, you fool," he yelled. "You should have made a reservation. Already we've two families in every room. Downstairs there isn't even floor space for a sleeping mat."

Just then a contraction came.   "AAARRRGH!"

The innkeeper looked up at me, his anger reddening his face. "Why did you bring a pregnant woman on such a journey? Where are your wits, man?"

"It doesn't matter what you think of me," my dearest Joseph pleaded. "We have to have a place for the night. The baby is coming!"

The innkeeper's wife, standing close behind him, reached out and jiggled his sleeve. "There's the stable out back," she suggested. "At least they'll have some privacy there."

At that point, I just wanted a place for our baby to be born. We followed the servant to the stable door. Joseph helped me down from our donkey. He reached out and gently brushed my hair from my face.

"I'm sorry, Mary," he whispered. Tears slipped down his cheeks as he wrapped his arms around me. He leaned his forehead against mine and prayed: "*Most holy God, we need your help tonight. We thank you that we have been offered this stable. Give Mary strength and courage for the birth. Keep her and the child strong and healthy. We thank you for the honour of being the parents of your precious child, Jesus. Amen*"

I felt God's peace settle in my heart as he whispered the words.

The innkeeper's wife, Dora, sent one of their servants with food and blankets. He helped Joseph spread fresh clean straw in an empty stall, then left us alone. Using some of the straw, Joseph made a soft bed in the manger in preparation for our Jesus.

We lay down together, and listened to the rustle of the animals' movements as they slept. Joseph held me when the contractions came. My mother's wisdom about acceptance came to mind. *When we stop fighting what is happening, we can begin to find the good things in life.*

"This is much better than all the noise and people in the inn," I said. "The warmth of the animals has driven the chill from the air. I have always loved animals. They don't judge you or make fun of you." In the silence of my heart I prayed: *All things are possible with you, most holy God. Thank you for this place.*

The birth pains were coming closer together when Dora appeared with a jug of fresh water.

"I'm a midwife," she announced. "I'll stay until the child is born."

"Thank you," we both said at the same time. "Thank you."

Dora knew exactly what to do. I worked hard. It seemed like a long time, but it really wasn't. I only had a few hours of hard labour, and then our Jesus was born. Dora told me that I did well. I needed to hear that.

Now, he's here. Our precious Jesus is with us. I can hardly believe that he's finally here. There are no words to describe my joy. Isn't he beautiful?

There is light streaming through a window high above our heads, enveloping us in a golden glow. Joseph tells me, a star, the brightest star in the sky, is shining down on us. I feel as if that wonderful starlight has filled my heart. Being a parent is an awesome responsibility It's an even greater responsibility to be the mother of the Messiah.

I looked into our Jesus' eyes and promised him, "You're so tiny and helpless. I'll protect you from people's miserable words. I won't let them hurt you as they hurt me. I don't want you to suffer ever. You've such a big job ahead of you...Jesus, I know you'll have to walk your own life journey, but I don't want anyone to hurt you. I love you Jesus. Already, I love you..."

I prayed: *Please God care for him, care for our Jesus...Thank you God for the blessing of this wonderful child. Isn't he beautiful?*

*****

Reflection

This year as you prepare for Christmas, remember that you are celebrating the birth of Jesus, God with us. Open your heart to receive God's unconditional love through him. Remember God came to earth as a baby, fragile and vulnerable, because God knew that we just naturally love babies.

CAN I HOLD HIM?

CAN I HOLD HIM?

The Birth of Jesus
Luke 2: 1-7

"In those days Caesar Augustus issued a decree that a census should be taken of the entire Roman world. 2 (This was the first census that took place while[a] Quirinius was governor of Syria.) 3 And everyone went to their own town to register.

4 So Joseph also went up from the town of Nazareth in Galilee to Judea, to Bethlehem the town of David, because he belonged to the house and line of David. 5 He went there to register with Mary, who was pledged to be married to him and was expecting a child. 6 While they were there, the time came for the baby to be born, 7 and she gave birth to her firstborn, a son. She wrapped him in cloths and placed him in a manger, because there was no room in the inn."

Introduction:

As a child I struggled to understand why the innkeeper would turn away Joseph and Mary. It always seemed mean. Over the years life experience has taught me to think about people and try to understand. We need to search out the back story in order to try to understand the actions of others. We don't know what has been happening in a person's life that could be affecting the choices they make. When I thought about the innkeeper's actions, my imagination led me to this story.

"CAN I HOLD HIM ?"
The Innkeeper's Daughter
Tells Her Story.

I saw him! I talked with him! Jesus, the great teacher and healer from Galilee. He's wonderful. He teaches with such passion about God's love and forgiveness. My heart soared as I listened to him. Jesus cares about all of us, even the children. He laughed with such joy as he listened to their stories. He took them in his arms and blessed them. Jesus is truly wonderful. They are saying that he is the promised one, the Messiah who is described in our Holy Scriptures. I believe it's true. Oh, yes, I do.

Actually, I've known for a long time that this man named Jesus was the Messiah. I learned about him on the night he was born. It's been more than thirty years, yet the memory is so vivid it seems like only yesterday. Let me tell you about it.

That particular year, Caesar Augustus had decreed that everyone should return to the place of their birth to be registered for the tax. Bethlehem was teeming with people. Our business had doubled. I remember my father, the innkeeper, rubbing his hands together in satisfaction and saying, "Thank you, Caesar, thank you," as he scurried around the inn.

The night Jesus was born, loud boisterous men filled our inn. Sweating bodies surrounded me, each one demanding something. I was up before dawn, fetching and carrying, preparing food, washing dishes. I thought the day would never end.

As I cleared away the evening meal, I heard a persistent pounding on the door. "Who is it now?" I wondered. I tripped over someone's outstretched leg and almost fell as I struggled through the people to the door. I wrenched it open and without looking up shouted above the din, "No room. We're full." I tried to slam the door shut, but there was a giant foot in the way. Only then did I look up and see them. A beautiful young woman, great with child, sat on a donkey. She winced with pain. The man reached out and grabbed my arm, his eyes wild with desperation.

"Get your master!" he commanded.

I knew what Father would say, but I had no choice. I shrugged off his arm, turned on my heel and yelled, "Father! Father!", as I threaded my way through the crowd toward the kitchen. Out of the gloom and smoke, Father appeared at my elbow with Mother standing close behind him.

"What is it?" he roared above the din.

I put my mouth to his ear and shouted, "There's a couple at the door wanting…

"There's no room. We're full," he interrupted. Then, pushing me aside, he stomped off towards the door muttering to himself.

I turned to mother and pleaded, "Isn't there some way we can help them? The woman is going to have a baby."

"Get back into the kitchen, the dishes are piled high," she scolded. A tear slipped down my cheek. Mother reached out with her apron and wiped it away. "My sweet Hannah," she sighed and hurried off after Father. "I'll try," she called back over her shoulder.

I washed dishes for what seemed like hours. It was midnight when mother returned.

"They're in the stable," she announced. "Baby's born...a boy." She picked up the mop. "Both mother and child are strong." she said and began to clean the floor. Smiling with satisfaction, she added, "You've done enough for today, Hannah. Go to bed."

I slipped out the back door away from the heat and the stench. I needed some peace and fresh air before sleeping. Above me, stars danced across the night sky. One in particular, much brighter than all the rest, shone down on our stable.

Into the silence came the baby's cry, a strong healthy wail. Curious, I ran to the stable. As I stepped inside, I could feel the warmth of the animals, and hear the rustle of their quiet movements. In a circle of starlight I could see them. The man held the baby close to his heart, comforting him with a gentle lullaby. The woman rested on the straw covered with the yellow blanket from my parent's bed. The man looked up and smiled as I stepped into the light. "Welcome," he said, his voice soft and gentle. "Have you come to see our beautiful baby Jesus?"

"Oh yes," I whispered.

"Please sit down," the woman said. "My name is Mary, and this is Joseph."

Her voice was so sweet. It reminded me of the tinkle of the temple bells. "I'm Hannah, My father owns this inn," I said proudly, as I settled down into the straw.

"Thank you for sharing your stable." Joseph said. "Your mother has been wonderful. My Mary needed her. We give thanks to God for your mother."

Joseph brought the baby over to show me.

"Can I hold him?" I asked.

He placed the baby in my arms. He was so small and vulnerable. He snuggled down close to my heart as if he belonged there. When I touched his tiny hand, his wee fingers opened up like a flower, and wrapped around my little finger. He held on. He actually held on. He opened his eyes and looked right into my soul. I felt enveloped within God's love. I knew in my heart even then that this was a very special baby. I wanted to hold him forever.

Mary's voice rang out in the stillness, "An angel told us that our Jesus is the promised Messiah. He will be a

Saviour, God with us."

I believed Mary then. I believe her today. Now Jesus is grown. He preaches with such wisdom and love. When he looked at me yesterday, I felt God's presence stir within me.

He said, "All people are God's beloved children, all people, not just the ones we find easy to love." He looked right at me and commanded, "Love all of God's children, everyone you meet, everyone. Hold them in your heart, for even your enemies are God's creation."

Of course I agreed to do as he asked. Thirty years ago, I held him as a baby, and he entered my heart. He's never left. I'm sure he has been with me ever since. I can do as he teaches. I am so grateful that I followed the star to the stable that night when I was thirteen.

*****

Reflection

God came among us as a baby because God knows that holding a baby inspires us to love.

Take a moment right now, to imagine you are the innkeeper's daughter. Close your eyes and see yourself standing at the stable's open door. See the star's light flooding the stall. Step inside. Sit down in the hay. In your mind, lift your hands to receive the baby Jesus. Hold him close to your heart. Let God's love fill your soul.

CAN I HOLD HIM?

THE LAST SHALL BE FIRST.

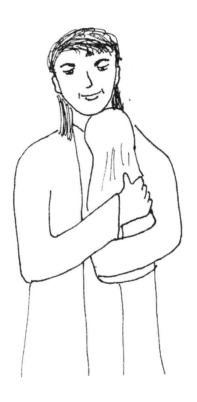

The Shepherds Come
Luke 2:8-20

"8 And there were shepherds living out in the fields nearby, keeping watch over their flocks at night. 9 An angel of the Lord appeared to them, and the glory of the Lord shone around them, and they were terrified. 10 But the angel said to them, "Do not be afraid. I bring you good news that will cause great joy for all the people. 11 Today in the town of David a Savior has been born to you; he is the Messiah, the Lord. 12 This will be a sign to you: You will find a baby wrapped in cloths and lying in a manger."

13 Suddenly a great company of the heavenly host appeared with the angel, praising God and saying,

14 "Glory to God in the highest heaven,

and on earth peace to those on whom his favor rests."

15 When the angels had left them and gone into heaven, the shepherds said to one another, "Let's go to Bethlehem and see this thing that has happened, which the Lord has told us about."

16 So they hurried off and found Mary and Joseph, and the baby, who was lying in the manger. 17 When they had seen him, they spread the word concerning what had been told them about this child, 18 and all who heard it were amazed at what the shepherds said to them. 19 But Mary treasured

up all these things and pondered them in her heart. [20] The shepherds returned, glorifying and praising God for all the things they had heard and seen, which were just as they had been told."

Introduction:

The shepherds' story of the night Jesus was born has always fascinated me. Even as a child I enjoyed playing hide and seek outside in the dark. A starry night sky felt magical. The night sounds were different. We were granted the privilege of being out after dark only in the summer, when people visited with children. I think my parents believed "there was safety in numbers." As an adult, I wanted to help children identify with this story, so I've told it from the point of view of a shepherd boy.

THE LAST SHALL BE FIRST
A Young Shepherd Tells His Story

The night the angel chorus filled the sky, I was just fifteen and shepherding a flock on my own for the first time. Being a shepherd is a lonely life. We look forward to those rare times when several of us bring our flocks together for the night. This was one of those nights.

Eight of us camped at the mouth of a ravine. Its steep, straight walls protected our flocks from wild animals and bandits. Our day's work done, we ate our meager supper. A damp, bone-chilling cold descended upon us as we huddled around the fire, sharing news and stories. The conversation eventually turned to talk of the Messiah, a Saviour for our people.

Uncle Elias started it. "The soldiers harassed my Elizabeth and the children when they were in Bethlehem last week. We need the Messiah to come now and free us from these accursed Romans."

"The Messiah will never come. He's just a myth," Jacob, the oldest shepherd among us, declared. "You need to give up on those old stories, Elias."

The same old argument was starting again. I had heard it all before. Life will never change for shepherds, I thought. I tossed the last of my tea into the darkness and stalked off to my tent.

I lay awake listening to the murmur of the men's voices punctuated by the occasional bleat from the flocks, huddled together down in the ravine.

It wasn't long before Jacob's voice rose above the others. "Enough!" he said finality ringing in his voice. "If the Messiah does come, he'll be a great warrior, a descendant of King David. We're just shepherds, outcasts. We'll be the last to see the Messiah."

I heard the sizzle of something wet being dumped on the fire.

"It's time for sleep. We'll move the sheep towards home tomorrow."

Someone groaned. I heard their footsteps clomp off to their tents. Soon, all became quiet.

Shivering in my bed roll, my thoughts turned to kings. Maybe someday, I would be the keeper of the king's horses; maybe even the Messiah's horse.

In my imagination, I saw myself finely dressed and standing in the king's courtyard. I was holding the reins of a magnificent black stallion, his coat shining from my many hours of patient brushing. The Messiah strode toward me. His confidence, his strength surrounded me. He looked right into my eyes when his hands reached for the reins…

Baa, Baa…The pitiful sound of a lost and frightened lamb penetrated my thoughts. My dreams scattered. Reluctantly, I dragged myself to my feet. From the tent doorway, I could see the outline of a lamb in the darkness. "How did you get so far from the rest, little one?" I whispered, as I walked over and wrapped my arms around him. I could feel his body tremble with fear. I gently rubbed his back in an effort to calm him.

Baa, Baa, Baa… Baa, Baa, Baa…"

"That's your mother. She's worried about you," I crooned, making my voice as soothing as possible. The ewe's form took shape in the star light. I set her baby down, and he ran to her on wobbly legs. The ewe stretched her neck and nuzzled him in greeting. Together, they ambled back into the ravine.

I stared up at the star covered sky. Silence and peace crept in around me.

Swishshsh…swishshsh, …

What was that? Fear enveloped me. In the northern sky, a soft light appeared, just a glimmer at first, but growing rapidly. Directly above my head, the swishshsh and the gleaming light converged. It swirled, round and round. Gradually, a shape appeared… a person… wings… an angel…I heard the hushed whispers of the other shepherds. They too had wakened and were gathered around me. I could feel their fear.

The angel spoke. His voice thundered across the ravine. "Do not be afraid. I bring you Good News of great Joy that will be for all the people. Today, in the town of David, called Bethlehem, a Saviour has been born to you; he is Christ the Lord. This will be a sign to you: You will find a baby wrapped in cloths and lying in a manger." (Luke 2: 9-12)

Suddenly, angels surrounded us. Everywhere I looked, I saw them, standing, flying, swooping, their wings and gowns, shimmering with an inner light. They sang with heavenly voices.

"Glory to God in the highest and on earth, peace, goodwill to all people." (Luke 2: 14)

Their song finished. Their message given. They disappeared. It was over.

Down in the ravine, the sheep were bleating nervously. A fresh, new wind rustled in the scraggly shrubs. Still excited, I cried out, "Let's go to Bethlehem. Let's do as the angel said. We'll see the Messiah."

Jacob raised his hands in disgust. "Not on your life will I leave my sheep. I know we all saw them, but they weren't meant for us. The most holy God would never send angels to shepherds."

"I agree with Jacob," one of the other men chimed in. "I'm not going anywhere. Our job is to watch the sheep."

"We can't risk the bandits and wild animals," said another. "I'm staying here where it's safe."

"The Messiah will be born in the palace or the temple in Jerusalem, not in a stable...in that Godforsaken little Bethlehem...," another shepherd sneered.

"No," I wailed. "They were God's angels. Their message was for us." I turned to my uncle. "Please," I pleaded.

Uncle Elias grinned. I'm sure he enjoyed disagreeing with Jacob. "Why not?" he said, his face alight with the adventure. "Anyone else want to go for a walk with David and me? Bethlehem isn't that far.

Jacob shook his head in disgust. "Go, you fools. We'll do your work for you."

Only Abe and John joined us. As we walked, I searched the skies for angels. Never had I seen so many stars. The brightest one seemed to be moving...ahead of us.

By the time we trudged down Bethlehem's dusty street, the moon's position told us several hours had passed. "Look," I said and pointed. "See that star. Its light is touching that stable, behind the Bethlehem Inn." The four of us stopped and stared.

"That's where we'll find the Messiah. I'm sure," I declared.

In the darkness, I could just make out my Uncle Elias' frown. "Why?" he muttered, "Why us? We're only shepherds." He put his arm around my shoulders. "Be careful. We don't know who is in there. Some people are afraid of shepherds."

Through the stable door, we could hear a baby crying. We brushed off our clothes as best we could and entered. That same star shone in through a window high on the wall and bathed one stall with light. In it stood a man, rocking back and forth, a crying baby in his arms.

"Quiet now, my little one," he said. "You and your mother need to sleep."

Still, the baby cried. We stood, just outside the halo of light. The woman sat up in the straw, her eyes full of questions and fear. Uncle Elias stepped forward into the light. He bowed our traditional greeting and spoke, "My name is Elias. We're here because the angels came to us on the hillside and told us that your son was the Messiah, the Saviour for our people."

The woman's body relaxed as the man answered. "Welcome, my name is Joseph. This is Mary. We've seen the angel too. He gave us the same message. He told us that we were to name the baby Jesus."

Mary looked so young, not much older than me. My eyes rested on the baby. He's crying as if his tummy hurts, I thought. My hands ached to comfort him.

Mary looked at me and smiled. "What is it?" she asked.

"I...I...My name is David. My mother says that God has given me the gift of caring for others, especially babies. Please, could I hold your Jesus?" I stammered, and stretched out my arms.

My uncle gasped and reached out to yank me back.

Mary smiled and said, "It's all right. I understand." She turned to Joseph, "Give Jesus to David. Maybe he can help."

I stepped forward into the light. He placed crying, squirming Jesus in my arms. I lifted him up to my shoulder so that his tiny head snuggled against my neck. I held him close, rubbed his back, and walked back and forth. The halo of light that surrounded us grew brighter and brighter. Jesus stopped crying and burped. I laughed, and looked down into his little face. "Jesus, my Jesus," I said. "The angel told me you're my Saviour, my Lord." His warm tiny body felt so good and so fragile. He closed his eyes and went to sleep. God's peace enveloped me.

The others knelt by the manger. They told Mary and Joseph all about the angels' visit. Time passed. Their conversation ended. Uncle Elias looked up at me. "You'd best give the baby back," he said. "You've done what you came here to do. We all have."

I handed the sleeping Jesus back to Joseph. "Thank you," I whispered. "He's beautiful."

Mary's soft voice echoed mine, "Thank you."

A light breeze brought the scent of grass to our nostrils as we left Bethlehem. Over my head, the stars were magnificent. I may be only a shepherd, I thought, but I have this magnificent countryside. At the king's palace, there would be the noise and stench of the city. This life is good. You do care for us, Lord, all of us: even shepherds, I thought. Never again would I doubt the most holy God.

The sun was just peeking over the horizon when we came within hailing distance of our camp. "We've seen him. We've seen the Messiah," I called out as I ran up to the other shepherds. I stopped in front of Jacob. "You missed out," I said. I raised my hands up before him. "Look at these hands. They have held the Messiah. My hands have comforted Jesus. You said we'd be last to see the Messiah because we are just shepherds. I was the first, the very first!"

*****

Reflection

I offer this challenge to you, the reader of this story. As you prepare to celebrate Jesus' birth this year, keep your eyes open for God's angels. Have the courage and faith to listen for the Christ child's cries of hunger, loneliness, fear within the people you encounter on the street, in the hospital, nursing home, at work and even at home. You too can hold him as you hold them. God's hope for the world is in your hands.

CAN I HOLD HIM?

FOLLOW THE STAR

The Magi Visit the Messiah
Matthew 2: 1-12

"2 After Jesus was born in Bethlehem in Judea, during the time of King Herod, Magi[a] from the east came to Jerusalem 2 and asked, "Where is the one who has been born king of the Jews? We saw his star when it rose and have come to worship him."

3 When King Herod heard this he was disturbed, and all Jerusalem with him. 4 When he had called together all the people's chief priests and teachers of the law, he asked them where the Messiah was to be born.5 "In Bethlehem in Judea," they replied, "for this is what the prophet has written:

6 "'But you, Bethlehem, in the land of Judah, are by no means least among the rulers of Judah; for out of you will come a ruler who will shepherd my people Israel.'[b]"

7 Then Herod called the Magi secretly and found out from them the exact time the star had appeared. 8 He sent them to Bethlehem and said, "Go and search carefully for the child. As soon as you find him, report to me, so that I too may go and worship him."

9 After they had heard the king, they went on their way, and the star they had seen when it rose went ahead of them until it stopped over the place where the child was.

[10] When they saw the star, they were overjoyed. [11] On coming to the house, they saw the child with his mother Mary, and they bowed down and worshiped him. Then they opened their treasures and presented him with gifts of gold, frankincense and myrrh.[12] And having been warned in a dream not to go back to Herod, they returned to their country by another route."

Introduction:

As is often the case with our traditional stories, over the centuries the biblical story of the three kings, who came from the East to see Jesus, has been embellished. If we examine the Bible story carefully, we discover that it tells us three things about these three Kings.

1.   There were some who came – not just three
2.   They were wise but not necessarily kings.
3.   They came from the East after Jesus was born. There is no mention of when they came. The story in Matthew about Herod and the children could lead us to think they came sometime within two years of Jesus' birth.

Consequently, I have focused on the message of the story, and let my imagination fill in the details.

FOLLOW THE STAR
Melchie, The Third Wise Man

My name is Melchior ben-Alim, Melchie for short. My father and I study the stars and interpret their messages. People come from all over Egypt to hear the wisdom of my father, Alim. He is as rich and powerful as a king. Always I have yearned to be like him. When I was young, I scanned the heavens, night after night, searching for a new star. One cool clear night, it happened.

"Father, look, a new star," I exclaimed.

Father's ancient eyes could see nothing new. "You're imagining it, Melchie."

I didn't argue. No one argued with my father. Still, I was sure my new star was there. The next night it seemed a little brighter. I searched the writings of the sages. Someone must have foretold my star's appearance. By day, I searched for a prophecy. By night, I watched my star grow brighter. Seven nights passed. I opened a tiny scroll, brittle with age. The letters were faint. "Study the heavens. Watch. A new star will appear in the eastern sky to announce the birth of a king in Israel. He will bring new life to his people."

With shaking hands, I gave the scroll to my father. That night, even he was able to see my tiny star of the East, shining bravely down from the heavens. Together, we celebrated.

"What will you name it?" my father asked.

I frowned... "Star of the East."

Father nodded.

Every night, I imagined my precious Star of the East calling, "Follow me. Follow me."

"Follow you," I argued... "But I'd have to travel at night. There would be bandits...I can't do that. I want to claim you as my discovery, not follow you."

Still my star's call persisted until, thoroughly frightened, I confessed my distress to my father.

My father said, "Many years ago, before you were born, Melchie, I had a dream about a new star that would announce the birth of a very special king. For years, I've watched and waited. I planned to find that king. Now I'm too old. You will go in my place."

"Come with me," I begged. "I cannot go alone. I need your wisdom."

Father was adamant. "Son, this star is yours to follow."

"Follow my star, alone? Leave all that I've ever known, my comfortable life? I can't do that." I shook my head and walked away. My star's message dogged my every footstep. "Follow me. Follow me." I couldn't stand it. Finally, I surrendered and said to my father. "You're right, I'll follow my Star of the East."

He smiled, hugged me, "Thank you, Melchie."

I dawdled with my preparations. When I could put my departure off no longer, I embraced my father, tears of fear flooding my eyes. "I'm ready," I mumbled.

He whispered in my ear, "Melchie, my precious son, remember, you're making this pilgrimage for both of us. The gods will go with you." Reaching deep into the folds of his robe, he drew out a black velvet bag. With a flourish he retrieved a small cerulean blue glass flask. He held it high, turning it so that the star engraved in the side flashed in the last rays of the setting sun. "Take this," he commanded. "It contains my prophecy for the new king."

I wrapped several gold pieces in cloth and slipped them into the bag with father's bottle. Together, my father and I walked outside where my servant, Adar waited, holding the reins of our camels. I concealed the precious bag beneath my camel's saddle blanket. I inhaled deeply of the night air and mounted my camel. Leading two pack camels loaded down with precious gifts for the new king, Adar and I rode off into the darkness.

At the end of our fourth night's travel, the sunrise unveiled a miracle. We stopped, and stared. Water, endless blue water stretched to the horizon and merged with the blue sky. My eyes burned from the sun's reflection dancing off its mirror-like surface. We had reached the Mediterranean Sea.

When Adar shook me awake that night, the sea had become a vast undulating black carpet with a fringed hem where the waves broke upon the shore. For many nights, my Star of the East led us along the sea's dark shores.

As we entered the land of Israel, bandits waylaid us. Outnumbered, we fought bravely. They murdered Adar and left me for dead at the side of the road. Near morning, I heard a shuffling sound. *Had the robbers returned to finish me off?* I lifted my head. My camel, Serafina, came swaying from behind a thicket. She knelt down beside me, and nuzzled my shoulder. Grateful, I reached up and stroked her nose. She waited patiently, while I struggled into the saddle. Then, slowly, she rose to her full height. I clung to the saddle drifting in and out of consciousness. Serafina stopped in the courtyard of an inn. Gentle hands lifted me down and cared for me as I convalesced.

As my wounds healed, I kept vigil night after night arguing with my Star of the East. "My pack camels are gone. Adar is dead," I wailed. "All the precious gifts I had packed for the king are gone. Stop calling me. My journey is over."

Always the answer was the same. "Follow me. Follow me."

Once I was well enough to worry about money, I faced the problem of paying for my care. Everything had been stolen. How would I pay? I decided to speak with the innkeeper.

"My father is the well-known astrologer, Alim ben-Harmena," I said. "He will pay you. When I return home and tell him of your kindness, he will pay the cost of my care threefold. He will send a servant with the money," I assured him.

The innkeeper smiled. "Yes, I have heard of this great scholar. In our sacred writings it says, 'We are to love those who are foreigners, for we were once foreigners in Egypt.' (Deuteronomy 10:19) I have only done what my sacred writings require. I will trust you and your father."

One morning, a caravan stopped at the inn. A servant called out loudly, "We need a room just for the day. We'll be gone by tonight."

Curious about these rich night travelers, I sought their company at the evening meal. With Greek as our common language, I learned they were following my star. They believed this star would lead them to an infant king. They introduced themselves as King Balthazar and Caspar, the magi. They entertained me with stories of similar pilgrims they had met on their journey. Some had given up because they were afraid to leave their own country, some because they had been robbed like me, some because they thought the journey too long. Only these two had persevered. They had joined forces in Persia.
"Come with us," Caspar invited. "You've come this far. Don't give up now."

My mind whirled round and round. What will I do? Just as the sun was setting, I made my decision. I would join this caravan. There would be safety with new friends.

My star led us to Jerusalem. Of course, I thought, *the king will be born in this main city of Israel.* I whispered to Caspar, "How will we find the king here among all these people?

He shrugged his shoulders and grinned, "We'll ask. Someone will know,"

We did ask, any who could understand us, "Where will we find the new born King of the Jews? We have seen a star in the eastern sky that signaled his birth." No one could answer or perhaps would answer our question.

A priest seized my sleeve as we passed the temple gate. Gruffly he spat out, "His majesty King Herod summons you to the palace tonight. Come to the north gate, three hours after sun down. Knock three times. The password is 'magi'." Without another word, the messenger melted into the crowd

"We mustn't go," I insisted. "This is a trap. They told me at the inn that King Herod is crazy jealous. He has people beheaded on a whim!"

Balthazar ignored me. "We'll have a good meal while we wait," he said.

Several hours later, I trembled with fear as Caspar knocked on the palace gate.

A muffled voice demanded, "What is the password?"

Balthazar answered with authority, "Magi."

The door creaked open. We faced two rows of spear points.

"Come," a voice commanded.

On shaking knees, I marched between Balthazar and Caspar, past the soldiers. The gate clanged shut behind us. Out of the shadows stepped a tall man dressed in a white toga, carrying an oil lamp. He gestured for us to follow him. Through a maze of long halls, and up several flights of stairs, he led us. Our footsteps fell into the rhythm of the soldiers who marched behind us. "Balthazar," I whispered. "We'll be robbed and beaten and thrown into prison."

Balthazar just smiled and shook his head, "Melchie my friend, be brave. This is a wonderful adventure."

He believed he was far too important to be harmed by this minion king we were about to see. I wished that I had his confidence.

Our leader stopped in front of a pair of large, elaborately carved doors. He turned and stared right at me. "Prepare to meet King Herod," he thundered.

This is it, I thought. **We're doomed.** Holding my breath, I begged the gods for protection. Without a sound, the huge doors swung open.

"The Magi," our guide announced.

King Herod sat upon a magnificent throne. His golden robe fell in deep folds to the floor. Beautiful young slave women clung to his arms, sat at his feet, massaged his shoulders. His self-satisfied grin did not quite reach his eyes. "Welcome, my friends," he purred. "They tell me you seek a king of the Jews. You follow a star. When did it appear?"

Caspar put his arm around my shoulders and said, "Actually Melchie here, was the first to see it. He claims it appeared in the night sky over Egypt nearly seven moons ago. He says it was…"

"Let him speak for himself," Herod snapped. "You…Mellllll…what did he say your name was?"

I gulped, "Mah-mah-Melchior, your highness. My name is Mah-Melchior"

"Speak then, Mah-Melchior,"

"The n-n-new king's sussstar apuh-peared sahseven moons ago. It was very fufufaint at first. Mu-mu-my father cahcouldn't see it at all. He..."

"Enough. I've heard enough. I've information for you. Our prophet Micah proclaimed that a king will come from Bethlehem to rule Israel. Go to Bethlehem and find this child. Leave no stone unturned. As soon as you find him, send word to me and I'll join you at once."

"Yes, your muhmajesty. Tha-thank you for the help, your muh-muh-majesty."

Herod waved his handkerchief with contempt. "Leave us," he snarled. "Go. Go!".

Relieved, we turned as one and left the room.

Our escort rushed us to the gate. Once outside, I gulped the fresh air. *We're free, I thought. We still have our heads. I'm grateful.*

The trip to Bethlehem the next morning was short and uneventful. We rested at an inn while we waited once again for darkness, for our star to appear.

At dinner, Balthazar asked me, "What gift will you give this king? Everything you brought was stolen."

I held up the bag that had been hidden beneath my camel's blanket. With my father's flourish, I drew out the blue bottle with its star insignia.

"It's beautiful," Caspar exclaimed. "What's in it?"

Carefully, I removed the stopper and sniffed. I frowned in concentration and sniffed again...*bitter, bitter perfume? My father has given me myrrh, the sacred spice that is wrapped with the body when it is buried. My companions won't be impressed. What shall I say? My mind raced. Ahhhhh, yes.* I waved the sparkling bottle before their eyes. "I have brought precious myrrh, the spice of death. This is my father's prophecy. "The king will die as he saves his people. Myrrh brings sweetness to death. It is a good gift."

Caspar frowned. Balthazar just raised his eyebrows.

When we stepped outside that night, my star's light shone on the door of a humble, flat-roofed dwelling near the end of the street. Clutching my bottle of myrrh, I trailed down the street behind Balthazar and Caspar. Once again, Balthazar knocked. A tall, gentle looking man opened the door.

"We've come to see the king," Balthazar announced. "My name is Balthazar. This is Caspar and Melchior. We have brought valuable gifts."

The man nodded. "Welcome. My name is Joseph. Please enter."

He turned and led us inside. In front of the window, in a halo of starlight, sat a lovely young woman. Her long dark hair fell over her face as she gazed at her sleeping baby. That beautiful silver glow spread out into the room to include all of us. I felt surrounded by love, so strong, it seemed as if I could reach out and touch it. Peace reigned.

"This is Mary and our son Jesus," Joseph said. Mary looked up at us and smiled.

Balthazar stepped forward first and knelt down in front of her. He held out an embroidered bag. "Gold...gold, my gift for your tiny king."

Mary nodded and looked up at Joseph. He bent down and took the bag. "Thank you. This is needed," he said.

Caspar came next. His outstretched hands offered an intricately carved box of frankincense sealed with wax to preserve its fragrance. "For your son, the new king of Israel. Incense for one who is even greater than the high priest."

Again Mary nodded. "Thank you," she said, as Joseph received the box.

It was my turn. This was the end of my journey. I had travelled so far to find fame and fortune. Here in this tiny home, with these common people, I had found my king. I stepped closer and knelt down. The baby Jesus awoke, turned his head and looked at me. His eyes rested in mine. Peace flowed into my soul. "A king," I whispered. "You truly are a king. Your star, not mine, has called me from afar. Someday you will reign over all the world. You are my Saviour."

His mother flashed a smile at me. She spoke, her voice filled with love. "You know the prophecy. You know that my son is the Messiah, the Savior of our people."

I could only nod and hold aloft the bottle that twinkled in the star light. Mary took it and drawing out the stopper, she passed it beneath her nose. Tears came to her eyes. "You do know the prophecy," she breathed. "You know he will suffer and die for his people."

I nodded. "A suffering Saviour..."

"No, I don't want this to be true," she moaned, shoved the cork back into the bottle and dropped it onto the straw covered floor. She clutched Jesus tightly to her breast. "I will protect you," she whispered. "I will protect you."

My eyes filled with tears. I reached out to touch the head of baby Jesus. Words came to me from nowhere. "You will be a new kind of king," I prophesied. "You will be the king of love." I dropped my hand, and rose to my feet. "Come," I said to my friends. "We must go."

Back at the inn, we sat in silence for a long time, thinking about the baby and how it felt to be in his presence. It was late when we laid down to rest.

As sleep descended I heard Caspar say, "Tomorrow, we will go back to Herod in Jerusalem."

We slept.

In the middle of the night, I awoke, covered in sweat. I shook Balthazar and Caspar. "Wake up, wake up." I shouted.

"Go back to sleep," Caspar groaned.

"Listen to me," I ordered. "I've received a message in a dream.
Balthazar reached out to rub my back. "We're listening, my friend."

"An angel said, 'Don't go back to Herod. Go home a different way.' The angel said it over and over again. 'Go

home a different way, a different way, a different way.'
You have to believe me."

"Simmer down," Balthazar responded. "I've no intention
of returning to Herod. As soon as he gets the information
he wants, he'll dispose of us. Your angel is wise. We will
leave at first light. The sooner we're out of Herod's
territory the better. Now go back to sleep."

We were up and gone before dawn. We did return home
a different way. Actually, I've been traveling a different
road ever since. I left home in fear, to follow the star,
hoping to become an important and respected man.
Meeting the little king Jesus has changed all that. There
must be one God above all of our Egyptian gods. Never
have I seen the forces of nature come together to identify
a king. Never have I felt such love around me and within
me as I did that night in Bethlehem. His love has never
left me. I am so glad I had the courage for the journey.
Answering God's call has changed my life. I am sure, that
tiny king will make a difference in the world.

*****

This Year, After Bethlehem Choose a Different Way. Let Jesus Transform Your Life

CAN I HOLD HIM?

A GIFT FOR ALL PEOPLE

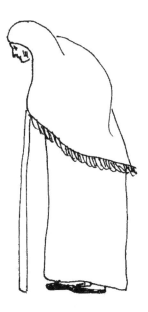

Jesus Is Presented in the Temple
Luke 2:22-38

"22 When the time came for the purification rites required by the Law of Moses, Joseph and Mary took him to Jerusalem to present him to the Lord 23 (as it is written in the Law of the Lord, "Every firstborn male is to be consecrated to the Lord"[a]), 24 and to offer a sacrifice in keeping with what is said in the Law of the Lord: "a pair of doves or two young pigeons."[b]

25 Now there was a man in Jerusalem called Simeon, who was righteous and devout. He was waiting for the consolation of Israel, and the Holy Spirit was on him. 26 It had been revealed to him by the Holy Spirit that he would not die before he had seen the Lord's Messiah. 27 Moved by the Spirit, he went into the temple courts. When the parents brought in the child Jesus to do for him what the custom of the Law required,28 Simeon took him in his arms and praised God, saying:

29 "Sovereign Lord, as you have promised,
    you may now dismiss[c] your servant in peace.
30 For my eyes have seen your salvation,
31   which you have prepared in the sight of all

nations:

³² a light for revelation to the Gentiles,
   and the glory of your people Israel."

³³ The child's father and mother marveled at what was said about him.³⁴ Then Simeon blessed them and said to Mary, his mother: "This child is destined to cause the falling and rising of many in Israel, and to be a sign that will be spoken against, ³⁵ so that the thoughts of many hearts will be revealed. And a sword will pierce your own soul too."

³⁶ There was also a prophet, Anna, the daughter of Penuel, of the tribe of Asher. She was very old; she had lived with her husband seven years after her marriage, ³⁷ and then was a widow until she was eighty-four.⁽ᵈ⁾She never left the temple but worshiped night and day, fasting and praying. ³⁸ Coming up to them at that very moment, she gave thanks to God and spoke about the child to all who were looking forward to the redemption of Jerusalem."

Introduction:

The dedication of Jesus at the temple is not a well-known story. We hear it but seldom spend time with it. It is an important story, for it reminds us that Jesus was born a Jew to devout parents. It tells us that Mary and Joseph kept the rituals of their faith. This story also tells us that along with the shepherds and the kings, temple leaders like Simeon and Anna also recognized the baby Jesus as the Messiah.

A GIFT FOR ALL PEOPLE
Gentile and Jew

My name is Anna. I am from the house of Phanuel and the tribe of Asher. I have spent my life at the temple, well, not quite all of it. I grew up at home and was married as all young girls are. My father was wealthy and powerful. He made sure that I was given in marriage to a strong, healthy, young man from an equally wealthy and powerful family. Nathaniel and I had seven good years together. We were a good match. He loved my thick, dark hair and enjoyed the fact that I was tiny, yet physically and emotionally very strong. Although Nathaniel was just a bit taller than I, he was sturdily built like a Roman column.

Even though our parents had arranged our marriage, we loved each other deeply. We were very disappointed that after five years of marriage, our love had produced no children. In our society, children are a sign of wealth and prestige as well as essential in our old age. I was barren. At the beginning of our sixth year, Nathaniel contracted leprosy. How, I'll never know. The disease is horrible. He was cast out into the catacombs. I was heartbroken. Thankfully it only took two years for him to die. I gave thanks to God for that mercy.

My father could find no one for me to marry. Nathaniel had no brothers. No amount of money can buy a husband for a barren woman. I pleaded with my father to let me go to the temple. That's all I wanted. I loved the temple. It was filled with peace and beauty. "Let me devote myself to prayer and fasting," I begged. "Use my dowry to buy me a place at the temple for life. I believe God is calling me to the temple." Finally, my father accepted defeat and did as I asked.

For sixty-two years I have served God here at the temple in Jerusalem. As I prayed and fasted I used my gift for needle work to make beautiful hangings and clothes for the priests. I polished all the elaborate carvings and statues. As a girl in my father's house, I had learned to read. I could study the scriptures. I could read the signs of the times. I listened to the priests and to other visitors to the temple. I listened most of all to the most Holy God. Women and children would come to me for advice. As the years passed I became known as Anna the prophetess. My wisdom and understanding were sought.

By the time Mary and Joseph brought Jesus to the temple, I had lived so long that I had become a legend. People did not see my wrinkles or my bent back. They did not see my tiny figure with its crown of graying hair piled high and wisps flying off in all directions. They only heard my voice, weakened and hoarse with age. They wanted my blessing, and my prophecy.

I have always loved the dedication ceremony for babies. Babies are God's gift of a new life. Over the years, I had held many babies. Each one was unique, and yet all were the same. As soon as a young couple named Mary and Joseph entered courtyard with their baby, I knew this child was different, special in a new way. I could see God's Spirit swirling round him and his parents.

It had been forty-one days since their baby's birth. Mary's time of purification was over. They came with the required two young pigeons, one for a burnt offering and one for a sin offering. They brought their baby Jesus to dedicate him to God.

I set down my knitting, and stretched out my hands, anxious to hold this child. Simeon stepped in front of me. Simeon, who wasn't even a priest, reached out and took the baby from his mother's arms. Yes, Simeon is devout. He comes often to the temple to pray. Always, he is laden with food for the priests, beautiful linens for the temple, sacrifices. Yes, he is respected, but still, the child was mine to hold. It is the custom here that the child comes to me first. I pulled at his sleeve, but he shook my hand away. "Leave me, Anna," he whispered. "You're turn will come."

What will these parents think? Simeon has no gowns of office."They will be afraid," I thought. I stepped toward Mary and touched her arm. I could feel her body trembling. "He will not harm your son," I reassured her. "He is Simeon, a most respected Jew. Listen to him."

Simeon, lifted the baby Jesus up towards the altar and said, "Sovereign Lord, as you have promised, you may now dismiss your servant in peace. For my eyes have seen your salvation, which you have prepared in the sight of all people, a light for revelation to the Gentiles and the glory of your people Israel." (Luke 2:29-32)

Mary and Joseph gasped with surprise. I could see that they knew their child was special, but they didn't expect anyone else to recognize that. Mary, reached for her baby, and Simeon spoke again, offering a blessing first on the child and then the parents.

He turned to the mother, and his voice thundered: "This child is destined for the falling and the rising of many in Israel, and to be a sign that will be opposed so that the inner thoughts of many will be revealed—and a sword will pierce your own soul too."(Luke 2:34-5)

Mary moaned. Tears slipped from her eyes as Simeon placed the child in her outstretched arms. "He will be a sign that will be spoken against," she whispered. She held him close to her heart as she shook her head. Over and over again, she whispered, "No, No, I will not let anyone harm you. I will protect you."

I stepped in front of her and wiped the tears from her cheeks. She looked at me with such trust. Then she placed the baby in my arms. I could feel the Spirit surround me. "Thank you God," I cried out. "Thank you God." I turned to the crowd that had gathered. For the first time in years, my voice rang out strong and clear, "This is the child God has given us for the redemption of Israel. This is the Messiah who will bring freedom from sin to our people." I would have danced, but at the age of eighty-four, my legs are no longer strong. I hugged the baby close to my heart and asked God's blessing on him. Then I gave him back. She smiled at me, and they went to the priest.

My moment was over, and yet it will never be over. My life is finished. I have done what I was born to do. I have identified the Messiah. Thank you God. I will not be alive to know if Simeon's prophecy is true. I do know that this child will walk with God every day of his life. This child will do great things. This child will bring freedom to all people just as Simeon predicted.

*****

This child is a gift for everyone, even you.

CAN I HOLD HIM?

THE REFUGEES

The Escape to Egypt
Matthew 2:13-20 (NIV)

"13 When they had gone, an angel of the Lord appeared to Joseph in a dream. "Get up," he said, "take the child and his mother and escape to Egypt. Stay there until I tell you, for Herod is going to search for the child to kill him."
14 So he got up, took the child and his mother during the night and left for Egypt, 15 where he stayed until the death of Herod. And so was fulfilled what the Lord had said through the prophet: "Out of Egypt I called my son."
16 When Herod realized that he had been outwitted by the Magi, he was furious, and he gave orders to kill all the boys in Bethlehem and its vicinity who were two years old and under, in accordance with the time he had learned from the Magi. 17 Then what was said through the prophet Jeremiah was fulfilled:

18 "A voice is heard in Ramah,
weeping and great mourning,
Rachel weeping for her children
and refusing to be comforted,
because they are no more."

19 After Herod died, an angel of the Lord appeared in a dream to Joseph in Egypt 20 and said, "Get up, take the child and his mother and go to the land of Israel, for those who were trying to take the child's life are dead." "

Introduction

The world has so many refugees. We hear about them, and now, we see them on our city streets. Often, we don't consider what their lives are like. We forget that they might be homesick even in the midst of their gratitude for safety. We must never forget that Jesus and his family lived for a time in Egypt as refugees. Listen as Mary tells her story of that time.

THE REFUGEES

We're here, and we're safe. I'm getting used to it, and yet still I long for home. If I had only known what the future held that night when the angel Gabriel told me about Jesus, would I have said yes so easily? Maybe not, and yet we have our child Jesus, beautiful, wonderful Jesus. Even in the midst of my pain, I am glad I said yes.

When I think about that night, I remember being so excited, so honored. I was the chosen one. My child was to be the Messiah. I hold that memory close, especially the angel's words, "With God, all things are possible." But you have already read that story. This story is about what happened after, after his birth, after the shepherds came, even after the Wise Men.

When the Wise Men left, Joseph and I looked their gifts over carefully. I remember untying the thong of Balthazar's pouch made of pliable inlaid leather. Joseph's huge calloused hand barely fit inside it. His dark eyes filled with wonder as he drew out, one at a time, five gold pieces, drachmas they're called in Egypt. They glistened in the lamp light as he laid them on the table.

"What will we do with them?" I asked Joseph. "No one will believe that a foreign king brought them for Jesus. We'll be accused of stealing."

Joseph shook his head as he gathered them up and put them back into the pouch. "When we need them, God will show us what to do," he said.

That night I couldn't sleep. I tossed and turned. The moon had begun to sink towards the western horizon when I threw back the blankets and rose from our pallet. Shivering in the cold night air, I stared out the window at the sliver of new moon hanging low in the sky. I whispered:

"Most holy God, the Wise Men said our Jesus would be a great king and an even greater priest. That sounds so wonderful. Why did the young one, Melchior, bring Myrrh? He said our Jesus would die saving his people. Please protect our Jesus. Keep him safe with you.

Eventually, I fell into bed exhausted and cuddled up to Joseph's long, warm body, seeking solace and peace.

In the morning, Joseph awoke very agitated. "We must leave today," he said.

"Why?" I asked. "I thought we planned to make our home here in Bethlehem."

"Last night I had a dream. Once again the angel Gabriel came to speak to me. He said, "Herod is searching for our Jesus. Herod is a jealous king. He wants our Jesus dead…We must go to Egypt…Mary, sweet Mary, Jesus is in danger. We must leave immediately."

Frightened, we gathered our few belongings into sacks. Down into the middle of the biggest one, Joseph put the Magi's gifts. He paused as he dropped Balthazar's pouch of gold into the sack, "At Gaza, we'll find my old friend Asa. He will help us. He will know what to do with these coins."

We went to the market to buy food for the journey. Joseph chose to buy a second donkey. It took most of our money. I worried that we would not have enough to go all the way to Egypt. I remembered the angel's words, "With God, nothing is impossible." Early the next morning we joined a caravan heading west towards the coast and Gaza.

After two days' travel, a tall, bearded man dressed in black, riding on horseback, caught up with the caravan. He brought terrible news.

"Herod is on a rampage. He believes that within the last two years a child has been born in Bethlehem that is to be King of the Jews. Herod will not be replaced. He has ordered his soldiers to kill all the baby boys born there within the last two years. Herod made no announcement. Soldiers just appeared in Bethlehem and started the slaughter. Many have run away. The soldiers are out searching for them. They cannot escape."

I shuddered with fear and pulled Jesus closer to my heart.

Joseph whispered in my ear. "We'll be safe. God is with us. Two more days and we'll be at the coast."

"Are the soldiers coming this way?" I asked Joseph?

The messenger heard my worried whisper. He looked straight at me. His eyes were kind. "At the moment, Herod's soldiers are combing the area between Bethlehem and Jerusalem. They believe no one has had time to join a caravan, so they haven't turned west yet.

Maybe they won't."

That night Joseph and I and Jesus huddled together under the stars. Wrapped in blankets, we prayed, *"Most holy God, give us courage. Nothing is impossible with you. Bring us safely into Egypt.* Then we prayed for the people of Bethlehem. We cried together for their pain. Every time I nursed our Jesus, I thought of the mothers and their grief. *"Why, why?"* I pleaded with God. *"Why do you let such horrible things happen? Why does Herod live? What evil has overtaken him? What have these parents done? Why?"*

Joseph pulled us close to him. "There are no answers. We'll never understand. We can only trust in God," he said and sighed.

Each day we rode in fear. It was blistering hot. We were grateful. Maybe the heat would keep the soldiers away. At night we shivered in the desert's cold. Would we never reach the sea?

After four terrifying days, we finally reached Gaza. As we melted into the people of the city, we felt safe, at least momentarily. Egypt was still many long miles away. Joseph searched for Asa, his childhood friend. It had been many years since Asa's family had left Nazareth. Still we hoped we would find him. Already we needed to change at least one of the gold coins.

The morning after we arrived, Joseph went to a synagogue to ask for Asa or any of his relatives. God was obviously taking care of us. With Joseph's first question, he learned that Asa was a respected elder in a neighboring synagogue. The helpful rabbi gave him directions to Asa's home. That afternoon we visited him.

Asa and his family welcomed us and invited us to stay with them in their crowded household. Asa, his wife, and four children lived with his parents. He had named his eldest child Joseph because he treasured his childhood friendship with my Joseph. Asa arranged to change one of the gold coins to denarii. We would have enough for several years. My Joseph was sure he could find work in Egypt. He believed there is always work for carpenters.

We stayed with Asa for several days, awaiting a caravan leaving for Alexandria. Asa said that there were many Jews living there who could employ Joseph. Besides, Alexandria is a huge city. We would be safer there. I wanted to stay in Gaza, but we trusted the angel's directions.

We connected with another caravan, and once again set off for Egypt. Keeping up proved difficult with a toddler. At least the level coastal plain made travel easier.

I was exhausted, yet grateful to God when we finally arrived in Alexandria. Everything felt strange in such a big, bustling city. Asa had directed us to the southern Jewish quarter.

"Our Jewish kin will help you," he assured us. I'll never forget the love and concern in Asa's face as he handed my Joseph a note to a carpenter friend. "Speak with Abinajab," Asa said. "He'll help you find work or may even have work for you."

We searched out a place to live in that Southern corner of the city. Abinajab had work for Joseph. Gradually settled down into the familiar routine of family life.

A year has passed, and we have connected with a few other Jewish families. I have new friends, but still I long for home. At the market I hear so many strange languages, see people of every race. I miss my family. The people of Nazareth may have been mean, but at least I knew them. At times, I feel as if Joseph and I are a lonely island in the middle of a vast ocean of strangers. I find solace with God and with our sweet little Jesus. To be a mother is a wonderful blessing.

I'm sure that someday we'll be able to return to Nazareth. In the meantime, I have to trust in God and keep focused on the angel Gabriel's words, "Anything is possible with God."

*****

Reflection

We don't often think of Jesus, Mary and Joseph as refugees, but they were. I'm sure they experienced much of the trauma and the pain that refugees have live through today.

CAN I HOLD HIM?

AN ANCIENT LOVE STORY

The Boy Jesus at the Temple
Luke 2: 41-52

"41 Every year Jesus' parents went to Jerusalem for the Festival of the Passover. 42 When he was twelve years old, they went up to the festival, according to the custom. 43 After the festival was over, while his parents were returning home, the boy Jesus stayed behind in Jerusalem, but they were unaware of it. 44 Thinking he was in their company, they traveled on for a day. Then they began looking for him among their relatives and friends. 45 When they did not find him, they went back to Jerusalem to look for him. 46 After three days they found him in the temple courts, sitting among the teachers, listening to them and asking them questions. 47 Everyone who heard him was amazed at his understanding and his answers. 48 When his parents saw him, they were astonished. His mother said to him, "Son, why have you treated us like this? Your father and I have been anxiously searching for you."

49 "Why were you searching for me?" he asked. "Didn't you know I had to be in my Father's house?"[a] 50 But they did not understand what he was saying to them.

51 Then he went down to Nazareth with them and was obedient to them. But his mother treasured all these things in her heart. 52 And Jesus grew in wisdom and stature, and in favor with God and man."

Introduction:

There is very little information in the Bible about Jesus' growing up years. The one story found at Luke 2: 41-52 tells about an experience Jesus had when he was twelve. In the story, Jesus' response to his parents, "You know I must be about my Father's business." Seemed uncaring. It was as if Jesus was ignoring his parents' concern. It helped me to identify with Mary and Joseph as parents. It seemed to me that this is one of the times that "Jesus increased in wisdom and stature and in favour with God and humankind." (vs.52) Sometimes, we forget that Jesus was human as well as God with us. He grew and learned like all children.

As I thought about this story, the following conversation between Jesus and Joseph slowly formed in my imagination. My story takes place in Joseph's carpentry shop where Jesus worked with his father learning his trade.

AN ANCIENT LOVE STORY
Jesus Learns a Lesson

The day after their return to Nazareth, Joseph and Jesus started work in the carpentry shop at dawn, as was their custom. By mid-morning, their carpenter's aprons were smudged with dirt and dust, their shirts wet with sweat. Joseph set down his hammer. Wiping his glistening forehead with the back of his arm, he turned to his young son and said, "Jesus, it's time to rest a while. Come, let's sit outside in the garden." He picked up the stone jug that waited in the coolness of the wall's shadow. After pouring a cup of precious water for them to share, Joseph continued, "We need to talk."

Jesus nodded. He had learned long ago that "having a talk" meant his father was troubled. Silently, his mind reran the last few days. *What have I forgotten to do?* Jesus thought.

"I think you already know that your mother and I were upset when we finally found you in the temple the other day. I don't think that you truly understand our fear and panic. Instead of a lecture, I'm going to tell you a story."

Joseph was silent for a few moments. *We truly love this child*, he thought. *God promised us he would be totally God's child…and he is. It's so important that he understand. He must be compassionate in every situation.*

Joseph took a drink and began. "The first time I saw your mother, she was a baby, just two days old. Her grandmother placed her in my arms, and my heart filled with wonder as I gazed at this tiny bit of humanity. She opened her big brown eyes and looked up at me with total trust. When I touched her hand, she opened her tiny fingers and grasped one of mine. Her grip was strong for one so tiny. At that moment, I promised her that I would always care for her and protect her.

When she turned four, as is our custom, your mother was promised to me in marriage. I waited willingly. We became close friends. It was wonderful watching her grow and become a beautiful young woman. Always, I did everything I could to protect her. When she was fourteen, we were betrothed. That meant in one year we would be married. We were both very happy. A few months passed." Joseph paused to take another drink. He wiped his mouth with his apron.

One beautiful spring day, Mary came to me, her eyes aglow. "Joseph," she said, "I'm pregnant. An angel told me God has chosen me to be the mother of the Messiah."

Confused and shocked, I responded, "Pregnant...who has done this to you?" I thought someone had raped my precious Mary. I had failed to protect her.

Your mother innocently explained, "The Holy Spirit came upon me, just as the angel said." She looked at me with total trust. "What will we do?" she asked.

I had no answer. I knew that I couldn't marry her. Our custom says that a woman pregnant before marriage is a sinner and should be stoned. I couldn't do that to my Mary. "We will pray to God for wisdom," I said as I sent her home.

That night, I paced the floor, my heart filled with anguish, my mind in turmoil. "*God, what will we do?*" I prayed. "*No one will believe her story...I don't believe her. Help us,*" I pleaded. "*What happened, God? We cannot be married now...yet I cannot set her aside. I cannot cause her harm. I love her.*" Finally, I fell into a troubled sleep.

That night, an angel came to me in a dream, saying, "Fear not, Joseph, take Mary as your wife. Her child is from the Holy Spirit. The baby is the Messiah, the Saviour."

I was amazed. "It's true," I whispered. "Thank you, most holy God."

We were married quickly. As soon as it was apparent that Mary was pregnant, the mean, spiteful words began.

"Mary's damaged goods, Joseph. You were a fool to marry her. A real man would have her stoned." I tried to explain. We told them about the angel Gabriel. They didn't believe us. Over and over again, they mocked us.

"Why would God choose you, Joseph, a simple carpenter, and young Mary, to be the parents of the promised Messiah? Surely you can create a better story than that."

Laughter dogged my footsteps. My carpentry business slowly shriveled.

"That Joseph," they said, "he's not reliable. It's obvious Mary was pregnant before the wedding."

My heart ached. I had promised to protect your mother. I was a failure. When the decree came from Herod that we must return to our birthplace to register for the tax, it was nearly time for you to be born, Jesus. Your mother pleaded to come with me.

"Mary," I said, "Bethlehem is at least five days travel. The birth will be soon. You'll need your mother when the baby comes." My heart still aches when I remember her answer.

"Joseph, the ridicule here is awful. People are mean. Now that I am great with child, I am an embarrassment even to my mother. Don't leave me behind." As the tears rolled down her beautiful cheeks, she declared, "I'll be fine. There are midwives in Bethlehem." Then she smiled through her tears, "I'll be safe with you. You'll take care of me."

I have never been able to say no to your mother. I love her.

We travelled slowly. I tried to make it as easy for her as possible. We had hoped to stay with relatives along the way, but our reputation had preceded us. Uncle Jacob was the only one who gave us shelter. Even he begrudged it. What a terrible night that was.

By the time we reached Bethlehem, we were exhausted. All the relatives declared their houses were full. I was angry with them and angry with myself. *If only I had come alone, lodging wouldn't matter*, I thought. In my mind, I shook my fist at God and yelled, "*My God, my God, why have you forsaken us?*"

Your mother cried out with the first birth pain. "Joseph, my time has come," she gasped. "We must have a place."

She looked so tired and frightened. "There's an inn just ahead. They'll have a room. I'll make them rent us a room," I said with a confidence I didn't have.

I pounded on the inn door. A young servant girl answered.

"We're full," she said, so simply and easily, as if we didn't matter at all.

"No!" I shouted. "You have to have a room for us. My wife's exhausted. The baby is coming tonight." She tried to shut the door, but I had my foot blocking it. "Get your master," I demanded. Only then did she actually look at us. She turned and ran, leaving the door open.

The smell of sweat and smoke poured out. I peered inside. The room was filled with men, laughing and shouting. The noise was deafening. This was no place for my precious Mary.

"*Holy God, help us*," I whispered. The innkeeper appeared out of the murky noise with his wife at his heels.

"We've no room," he shouted. He looked at Mary. First shock, then anger registered on his face. "She's with child…You fool. We have no room. Hear me, man. We have no room."

Your mother cried out with another birth pain, "ooooooohhh…!"

"It matters not what you think of me," I pleaded. "Help us. Please." The innkeeper's wife tugged at his sleeve. She whispered in his ear. He turned to us.

"Dora suggests the stable. At least you'll have some privacy there. I'll send a servant to show you the way."

Dora reached out to your mother and patted her arm. "I'll be along in a little while to help with the birth, my child," she said, her voice filled with compassion.

Arm in arm, Mary and I followed the servant to the stable. "We'll be fine, just fine," I said over and over again, trying to reassure both of us.

Silently, I berated myself. *The innkeeper's right. I'm a fool. I'm worse than a fool. My beautiful Mary trusted me. Now, our child, the Messiah, will be born in a stable among the animals.* My heart cried out to God, *"I'm sorry, so sorry. Forgive me. Help me to care for her tonight."*

I'll never forget those next few hours. That stable, warm with the heat of the animals became an oasis of peace in the cruel world that surrounded us. A servant brought clean sweet smelling straw to make us a soft bed. I filled the manger as well, in preparation for you, Jesus. I held your mother as the birth pains came. High above us, the stars shone down through the only window. I remember one was much brighter than the others. As her pains grew stronger and came more often, that star grew brighter and moved closer till it filled the stable with light.

"Joseph, my beloved," your mother whispered. "God is with us. All is well." Her face radiated joy.

At that moment, I felt God's love and forgiveness rise up within me. Eventually, Dora came with blankets and food and everything we could need. She helped with the birth. We were grateful.

Your birth went smoothly. Dora was a midwife. She knew what to do. When Dora placed you, Jesus, in my arms, my heart soared with the wonder of new life, so small, yet perfect. I looked into your eyes and once again, made a promise as I had to your mother. This time my promise was different. Our Holy Scriptures say the Messiah is to be a man of sorrows, a suffering servant. I knew I could not protect you from all the troubles of life, but I could give my love and support to you. I could promise to teach you to trust in God, no matter what happens. So I looked into your eyes, and I promised to be the best father I could be.

I held you out to your mother, my precious Mary.

"He's beautiful," she said. "We won't let people hurt him as they've hurt us."

I responded, "Tonight Mary, God has cared for us. In the midst of our troubles, God has provided this place of peace. We know we can trust that no matter what comes, God will care for our Jesus as well."

We prayed, *"Thank you, God, for this place, for the animals that are keeping us warm, and for the compassion of the innkeeper and his family. Thank you for Jesus, your gift of new life to us. We trust that when our efforts to protect him fail, you will be with him. Praise you, most holy God. Amen."*

So Jesus, we promised you and God, long ago, always to take care of you. When we couldn't find you, we felt we had failed God. We knew you were not ready to take your place as the Messiah. We were afraid, afraid that someone had stolen you, would hurt you. When you responded to your mother's fear with, "Don't you know I must be about my father's business?", it felt like a reprimand. There was no compassion in your words or your voice. I want you to understand just how precious and special you are. I want you to know how much we love you. I want you to remember that even though your purpose in life is your priority, your family's love is important, too. You need to always have compassion.

Jesus nodded. His father's story had given him much to think about. This was a lesson he wouldn't forget.

*****

CAN I HOLD HIM?

THE RELUCTANT SHEPHERD

Introduction:

This story was inspired by my "church kids" at Dunsford United. They were just beginning to grow up (ages 12 and 13), when we introduced the digital projector to the congregation. Almost immediately, running the projector became the job of the oldest child in the Sunday School. It meant she could no longer leave the sanctuary with the rest of the children for Junior Church. This task soon became part of graduation from Sunday School.

THE RELUCTANT SHEPHERD

It's Christmas Eve. The church is packed with strangers, and I'm wearing Dad's old bathrobe. Mom's tea towel is fastened on my head with a rope. You guessed it. I'm a shepherd in the Church Christmas Pageant. I scanned the crowd and spied Eddy from my class at school. *Oh no*, I thought. *I'm too old for this and too tall!* I turned 13 last summer. How did I get myself into this mess? It's a long story.

Last September, I was ready to quit coming to church. It's not that church is awful or anything. In fact, I kinda like it. At least, I like Mr. Woolacott. He's my friend Jamie's grandpa. He always seems to find time to talk to me on Sunday mornings. He likes to tell stories just like my Papa. I miss my Nana and Papa. We moved here two years ago. Now, my grandparents live three hours away. We don't see them very often, so it's nice to talk with Mr. Woolacott.

Anyway, as I was saying, last September, I decided that I was too old for Sunday School and not old enough to sit through the adult service. I planned to stay home with Dad. He hardly ever goes to church, so why should I?

Then Mr. Green, the chair of property, called and asked to speak to me. That was a surprise. He'd never called me before.

"Kevin," he said, "the Harper's have bought the church a digital projector. Would you be willing to run the Power-point during the church service, please? You won't be the only one. We plan on having several people take turns. I'll be drawing up a schedule. Now that you're a teenager, I thought you might be willing to stay in church for the whole service."

I was pleased to be asked, but nervous about it, too. "Ummm," I said, "I dunno." I didn't want to tell him I had decided to quit coming to church altogether.

"I'd like you to think about it, Kevin, and pray about it," he said. "Talk it over with your parents as well. It is a big commitment. Our committee thinks you're old enough to take on the responsibility. Tell me on Sunday what you decide, okay?"

"Okay," I stammered. "I'll talk it over with my parents. See you on Sunday."

That was last September, and I've been running the projector ever since. There are other people on the list, but I like doing it, so I do it most of the time. I like being considered a grown-up and making a contribution. And I like sitting at the back in the sound booth with Mr. Woolacott. I thought I'd be safe from being in this stupid pageant. After all, I'm never in Sunday School.

Two weeks ago, Mrs. Rintoule, the Sunday School Superintendant, came and talked with me while I was putting the projector away.

"Kevin," she said, "I need your help. We're short children for the Christmas pageant. I know you no longer come to Sunday school, but we need a shepherd, one who's old enough to learn a few lines of dialogue and take care of the other two shepherds, the Kingley twins, Sam and Shelley. They turned three last week."

"But Mrs. Rintoule" I started, "I already have a job, I'll be running…"

She interrupted, "Greta Franklin said she'll run the projector for you. I really need you, Kevin. I've only got four children that are old enough for the main parts. Please."

"What about Jamie? Can't he lead the twins down the aisle?"

"I've already asked Jamie to be Joseph."

What could I say? I like Mrs. Rintoule. She's fun.

So here I am, with a twin on each side, walking down the church aisle and listening to the people sing, "While Shepherds Watched Their Flocks by Night."Sam's yanking on my hand. "What is it?" I whisper, just as the Christmas carol finishes.

"Look," he yells and points with his pudgy hand, "There's a big star."

The whole congregation laughed. I can feel the heat rising up my neck. I wish I was someplace else, anywhere else but here in this overcrowded church. I stare at the screen.

A huge star is pulsating. How did Mrs. Franklin get it to do that, I wonder?

The angel Gabriel, little Susan Filbert, shouts, "Peace on earth, goodwill toward men. To you is born this day in the city of David, a Saviour who is Christ the Lord. You will find him wrapped in swaddling clothes and lying in a manger."

Hey, I thought. *She did that very well. That was a big speech and she's only seven. Now, it's my turn.*

Shelley is yanking on my robe. She's crying. I lean down to find out what's wrong. "There's too many people. It's dark in here." She sobs.

I pick her up and say with as much enthusiasm as I can muster, "Let us go now to Bethlehem and see this thing that has taken place which the Lord has made known to us." Then we run right up to the front of the church. Well, Sam runs. I just walk fast because Shelley's heavy, and besides, Mom's never let me run in the sanctuary.

When we get to Joseph and Mary and the baby Jesus, Sam sits down right in front of the manger. I set Shelley down beside him, and then kneel.

The baby Jesus wrinkles up her little face and starts to cry. No, she wails… at the top of her lungs. She's Jamie's little sister, Melissa, born just a month ago. That's the neat thing about being born close to Christmas. It doesn't seem to matter whether you're a boy or a girl. All you need to be Jesus is to be a baby. Anyway, Melissa is yelling so loudly that no one can hear the narrator talk about the kings.

I look at Ashley, our ten year old Mary, and whisper. "Pick up baby Jesus."

"Oh no," Ashley whispers back. "Mrs. Rintoule said I was just to sit here and look peaceful and beautiful."

Behind me, the chuckles ripple across the church.

I turn to Jamie, who didn't want to be Joseph any more than I wanted to be a shepherd, and whisper a little louder. "She's your sister. Pick her up."

Jamie's eyes are huge. His face is white. No, it has a greenish tinge. He swallows and stares at his hands. I'm not sure whether he's afraid of his sister or the crowd, or he has the flu. It doesn't matter. *"God,"* I pray, *"make somebody do something. Make Melissa stop crying."*

Into my mind marches the thought, *Pick her up*. So I do. I put her on my shoulder and begin patting her back. That's what I've seen Jamie's mother do. "Sh, Sh, Sh, it's okay," I say to her very softly. I sit back on my heels and then roll over onto my bum, so I can rock back and forth. I begin to sing the only thing I can think of, "Silent night, Holy night…"Actually, I'm a pretty good singer. At least, that's what my mom says.

I'm all the way to "in heavenly peace," before Melissa shuts up. Sam reaches up and helps me pat. Three year old Shelley stands up and gives Melissa a kiss and then joins me with "Weep in hebbenwe pea."

I start to hum, and then I realize that the kings are at the front, and the narrator has stopped talking. All eyes are on Melissa and me. I hear the choir humming, too. Oh no! My microphone is still on.

Melissa squirms, so I lift her down from my shoulder and cuddle her close to my chest. Her hands are so tiny. She feels so warm and soft and alive. I look at her and say, "Jesus, long ago, you were just like this. Wow!"

"Joy to the world" comes blasting out of the organ, and everyone stands, even me. I hold the baby Jesus and sing to her, at the top of my lungs. "Joy to the world, the Lord has come." My smile is so big it feels as if it stretches right around the church. Joy, yes, Joy, Jesus is born. I look over at Mrs. Rintoule. "Thank you," I mouth. "I'm glad you asked me to be a shepherd."

It's all over, and Jamie's mom comes for Melissa. "No," I say. "We're fine. You take care of Jamie. I think he's going to throw up."

Sure enough, the words aren't out of my mouth two seconds when I hear him. What a mess! I shift Melissa back to my shoulder. I can't help, I crow to myself. I'm busy with the baby Jesus.

There's Mr. Woolacott heading my way.

"Merry Christmas," I say to him.

"Merry Christmas, Kevin. Thank you for being a shepherd. They needed you. Baby Jesus needed you. You took care of them all. And you sing beautifully. You made the Christmas story real for me. I'm glad you're my friend."

*****

CAN I HOLD HIM?

I'M AN ANGEL

Introduction:

I often hear congregational members say, "I wish we had more children in our congregation. How can we make it happen?" As you read this story, list the actions of congregational members that enticed this child to join. Talk about them with others. What is the financial cost of these actions? Are these actions happening in your congregation?

"I'M AN ANGEL"

My name is Ashley, Ashley Corinne Margaret Mary. Isn't that a mouthful? I think my mom and dad couldn't agree, so they gave me all their choices. They tell everyone that I am their special Christmas present because I was born on Christmas Eve, twelve years ago. Mom says I'm tall for my age. Dad calls me a bean pole and tells me to stand up straight. My hair is straight and black and smooth and shiny. My hair is the best part of me.

Oh, I forgot to tell you. I have a younger brother, Timothy. He's ten and half. He's little. In fact, the other kids call him "Timbit" because he's so small. He can skate, though. On the ice, his nickname is "Wheels." He streaks down the ice, in and around every one. Timbit's hockey games are both my parents' excuse when Grandma asks if we've started going to church when we're at home. We always go when we're at her house.

My parents split up last year. Timbit and I live with mom and go to dad's every other weekend and on Wednesdays as well. Dad lives on a farm about ten miles from us. At least life is more peaceful for both Timbit and me, now. My parent didn't exactly fight and yell like many parents. Instead, most of the time they didn't speak to one another. Anger filled the silence at our house. It was awful.

I know, I know, I talk too much. I haven't come to tell you about my family. I've come to tell you about being an angel. That's right, I was an angel in the church play last week, and it has changed me. I'm not exactly sure how, but I feel different.

It all began with my best friend, Vanessa. About a month ago, Vanessa came to school on a Monday morning all excited. Her Sunday School teacher had said that she would give out the parts for the Christmas play the next Sunday. Vanessa wanted to be Mary, the mother of Jesus. I had heard the Christmas story read at the Christmas Eve service in Grandma's church. It didn't sound that great. I was surprised that Vanessa wanted to be Mary.

"Aren't there any other parts for girls?" I asked.

Vanessa laughed at me. "Of course." she said. "Girls are angels and shepherds and sometimes even the Magi. It's just that I have never been Mary. Besides, the Cunningham's have a new baby, and she'll probably be Jesus. If I'm Mary, I'll get to hold her."

"How can a girl be the baby Jesus?" I questioned.

"Oh she can. Everyone's always happy to have a real baby, boy or girl. Besides, my Sunday School teacher, Miss Brown, says God could have come as a girl, but at that time, people were much more likely to listen to a man. They thought that women were supposed to stay home and take care of children."

"I sure am glad I didn't live back then," I said.

"Me too," said Vanessa. "Ashley, why don't you come on Sunday and be in the play, too. It's lots of fun."

"Oh no, I couldn't," I declared. "I don't know the story very well. I haven't been coming. Your teacher wouldn't give me a part."

"Yes, she would," Vanessa answered me. "Of course, she would. Everyone who comes gets a part. You can come the day of the play and be a shepherd or an angel. Now, if you want a speaking part, you need to be there this Sunday, and then come for the next three Sundays and to the Friday night practice as well. My mom says it's a big commitment."

"Oh, I'm not good enough." I responded wistfully.

"Ashley, that's not true. There are no auditions. You'll get a part, even a speaking part if you say you'll come. I'm sure Mr. Thoms will let you join the kid's choir as well. I sing in it. It's lots of fun too. Why don't you ask your mom to bring you this Sunday?"

"It is our Sunday with Mom... Oh, probably Timothy will have a hockey game... Well, I guess I can ask," I replied.

"Tell your mom that we will bring you if she can't. My parents are always willing to bring any kid to church," Vanessa replied. She sure was confident.

That's how it all started. When I asked, my mom sighed and said, "Let me check the hockey schedule." It just happened that Timothy's game was two in the afternoon. "What time is church?" my mom asked wearily.

"Nine thirty," I said promptly.

Mom groaned. "Well, you will have to check with your dad. I can bring you this Sunday, but will he be willing to bring you next week?"

"Ashley said that they would bring me if you couldn't."

"I am sure they would on the weekends you are here. They may not be so willing when they have to drive out to your dad's to get you," Mom responded. Sometimes I think Mom only sees the tough side of everything.

Well, I called Dad and surprise, surprise, he agreed. So we were set for Sunday. Timothy wasn't so sure he wanted to be a part of this, but he had no choice. I get dragged to hockey every week. This was his turn to be dragged somewhere for me.

I'll never forget that first week. There were only ten kids. Six of them were only four and three. Miss Brown was thrilled to have Timothy and me. After all, we can both read. Timmy didn't want a speaking part, so he was asked to be one of the Magi. Miss Brown said Vanessa could be Mary. Mary clapped and danced around. She was happy.

Miss Brown turned to me. "You're tall," she said thoughtfully. "How would you like to be the angel Gabriel? There are quite a few lines to learn. You would have to speak out clearly... Then she paused. Can you come for the next three weeks, Ashley?"

"Yes," I assured her. "I will be here even if I have to walk all the way from my dad's. I want a speaking part. Oh Miss Brown, thank you so much."

Miss Brown was obviously delighted. "We'll begin," she said, "by reading the whole Christmas story." She gave out Bibles, and we all took turns reading. I discovered that the Angel Gabriel had a big part in the story. Gabriel was there at the beginning with Mary and Joseph, and she was the leader of the heavenly host who came to the shepherds.

After Sunday School was junior choir practice. Timmy complained when mom agreed to stay. I was happy to think Mom would stay just for me. Well, she also wanted to stand and drink coffee and talk. She'd discovered that one of her friends went to this church.

Mr. Thoms is really nice. He had picked out three neat lively songs for us to sing during Advent and a beautiful lullaby for Christmas Eve. The songs were on a Karaoke machine so we could see the words on a screen. Mr. Thoms has a very loud voice, and he sang the songs one line at a time so we could learn them. We worked hard at choir practice, but I liked it. I love to sing. It makes me feel good. Afterwards Mr. Thoms came up to me and told me that I have a lovely voice.

"I hope you will be here next week," he said. "We need your voice and your enthusiasm. I'm glad you came today."

"I'm glad too, Mr. Thoms. I'm glad Vanessa invited me," I said.

When we went back to the church hall, Miss Brown stopped me and asked, "Ashley, where does your dad live?"

"Oh, he lives on a farm. Mom says it's about ten miles. Before I came today, my mom had me call and ask him if he would bring me. He said he would."

"Well, if you run into a problem, here is my phone number. Just give me a call. Either myself or someone from the church family can give you a ride."

"Oh Miss Brown, thank you," I said, "but I don't know if my mom will let me come with strangers." Right then, mom came along.

Putting her arm around my shoulders Mom said, "I overheard your offer, I'll make every effort to get Ashley here for the next few weeks. I can't promise after Christmas. I'll see. It would help to have your phone number, though."

As she handed Mom the slip of paper, Miss Brown said with a smile, "My name is Aileen Brown. My husband is the principal at Ashley's school." Mom looked relieved. I think she was glad to know something about Miss Brown.

I went home and practiced and practiced my lines. I had them all learned by the next Sunday. We were there every week. Dad came through with a ride for us when we were with him. He didn't seem to mind.

Being the angel Gabriel was fun. Mom came all three weeks and to the Friday night practice, too. She helped with the costumes. They needed a whole new costume for me because I am so tall. Mom went up to the attic and brought down a white filmy nightie that she had stored in a box. It was gorgeous. Mom said it looked just like something the Angel Gabriel would wear. Besides, it was much too fancy for wearing in bed. She and her friend made my wings, and I helped glue feathers on them. I even had a halo made of tinsel.

That evening I tried on the whole outfit, I whirled and danced around the living room, my wings flapping so gracefully. I felt beautiful. In that outfit, I am the angel Gabriel.

Vanessa had a lovely blue outfit as Mary and this pretty lace scarf to wear over her curly hair. Even Timmy enjoyed himself. His king costume was great. The crown was pretty big for his little head, but they lined it with cloth so it would stay on. He and dad made the little chest that was to carry the gift of gold for the baby Jesus.

The day finally came for the kids' service. We were all excited. There was so much noise in the church hall I couldn't hear my own voice. Even though there were lots of adults out there to help us, Dad took care of Timmy and Mom helped me.

When we were all dressed and ready, Rev. Maria appeared and raised her hand. First the adults, and then the children all raised their hands and stopped talking. Silence, wow. It felt as loud as the noise.

Rev. Maria said, "You all look wonderful. You're excited, and I'm excited, and so is God. The Christmas story is very special, and we love it. Today, you are the worship leaders. Remember that God is right here among us and within us. You can depend on God's help as you do your part. Know that God loves you, even when you make a mistake. What is important to God is that you are here and telling the story. Let's pray…"

It seemed to me that Rev. Maria was aglow. She always seems to glow. I am sure she has God's Spirit within her. We all trooped into the sanctuary. The church was full. My father sat in the very first row. My mother sat with her friend. I said my lines out clearly and loudly, just as Miss Brown had asked. It was easy because I believe the birth of a baby is Good News.

I want to keep coming to church. I like our minister, Rev. Maria. She asks us questions and actually listens to our answers. She's my friend. All the people at our church seem nice. I know enough people now that I can be sure of a ride on Sunday mornings, but I want my mom and my dad to come with me. They smile when they are at church. They need to know as I know, that God loves and accepts them just as they are, even though they don't live together anymore.

Yes, I am different now. I am not alone. God is with me and my church family is with me too. Thank you God.

*****

CAN I HOLD HIM?

THAT'S NOT YOUR BABY!

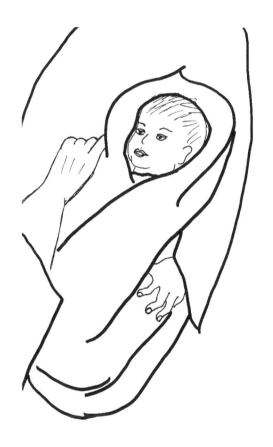

Introduction:

Christmas Eve monologues are fun. It has always been my goal to include as many people in leadership roles as possible. One Christmas Eve, a number of years ago, I drafted my youngest leader. She wasn't a congregational member. Her family didn't go to church. Still, both she and her brother led us in thinking about Christmas in a new way. This true story will always be written in my heart.

That's Not Your Baby!

"I've news. I've news!," my friend Christina said, as she slid her ample bulk onto the chair across from me. Her dancing eyes, and wide grin said it all. "Baby Diana was born at two a.m. this morning. She's three weeks early and she's tiny, but she's healthy and she's fine. I've been blessed with a second granddaughter."

Christina paused to give me time to congratulate her, and to let her eyes search the coffee shop to see if there was anyone else she knew. This proud Grandma wanted to tell the world. Finding no one, she continued with me. "Her name is Diana. She may be in hospital for a week or two until she gains some weight, but hopefully, she'll be home for Christmas."

Her announcement made, we talked of other things until Christina asked the very familiar question, "Are you ready for Christmas?"

"Well, sort of," I said. "I've written this monologue. I'm going to be Mary and tell her story. I'd like people to think about what it might have been like to be a teenager, unmarried and pregnant. Trouble is I need a baby, a very young baby, to be Jesus. We have only toddlers in the congregation. It will take about fifteen minutes to tell the story. A toddler is heavy and will squirm."

Christina's face lit up before I made my request. She knew what I was thinking.

"You'd like to borrow Diana, wouldn't you? You'd like my Diana to be Jesus on Christmas Eve."

I nodded.

"Wouldn't it be wonderful!" Christina said. "...Oh... well... Maybe not...I don't know. The kids don't go to church and they're over on the other side of the lake. They may not want to… I could ask though. It would be grand for Diana to begin life as the baby Jesus."

"I think babies that play the role of Jesus in Christmas plays received a special blessing," I said. "Go ahead and ask them. I can wait."

Our tea and muffin break finished, we rose to leave. "Give me a call as soon as you know," I said.

"I will," proud Grandma responded.

A few days later, the office phone rang. Christina's satisfied voice came over the wire, "They said yes. They think it would be neat for Diana to be the baby Jesus, as long as mom and baby are home from hospital and well enough. Could you handle not knowing until Christmas Eve day?"

"Sure," I responded. "I'll borrow Elizabeth's doll as a backup."

Christmas Eve dawned clear and cold. The sun shone all day. As evening came and the time for the worship service approached, Grandma called again. "We're coming. We're all coming. Diana's been home from hospital for three days, and they want to come. Isn't it wonderful? I'm so happy."

I hung up the receiver, my heart full of joy. Not only did I have a real baby for my story, but this family were coming to church together on Christmas Eve. What more could I ask of God?

The family arrived about fifteen minutes early, Mom, Dad, Grandma, three-year-old big brother, Tommy and of course, baby Diana, all dressed up in lace and bows. They marched right up to the front pew. All the rest were full. People do like to come to church on Christmas Eve. I welcomed them, shaking everyone's hand, even Tommy's, and made the obligatory remarks on the baby's beautiful outfit. Diana was the best-dressed Jesus I had ever seen.

The service started with a carol sing. The sanctuary was filled to the rafters. The lights were lowered, Candles flickered on the windowsills, on the communion table and in every other available spot, transforming the sanctuary into a magical kingdom. Entranced, the congregation settled into their pews, ready to hear the Christmas story once again.

Diana's father rose and handed me his precious child. Diana, of course sound asleep, was oblivious to her important role. I took her in my arms and smiled down at her lovely, peaceful face. I invited the congregation to join me in the preparatory prayer I say each Sunday just before I begin to preach: *"May the words of my mouth and the meditations of our hearts be acceptable in your sight, O Lord, our strength and our Redeemer. Open us to hear your Word for us today. We pray in Jesus' name. Amen."*

I raised my head, looked around at the expectant faces turned toward me, took a deep breath, bent down, kissed baby Jesus on the forehead and started my story.

"Just look at my baby Jesus. Isn't he beautiful." Once again I turned my eyes to baby Diana sleeping peacefully in my arms. "So beautiful," I said, "my baby…"

A small voice broke the silence in the church, "That's not your baby. That's my sister!" Three-year-old Tommy was not overcome by the magic of the moment. He was not about to be deceived. He knew who I was holding. How dare I claim his sister? Laughter erupted around the room. Tommy's little face wrinkled up and the sobs began. Once again amidst the sobs, he poured out, "That's my sister."

My heart filled with compassion. Quickly, I walked over to Tommy, bent down, putting little Diana as close to him as I could and said, "Yes, she certainly is. I've just borrowed her, Tommy. For just a little while, I'm pretending that Diana is the baby Jesus, and I am her mother Mary. It's a game of let's pretend."

He looked at me his eyes full of doubt, and sniffed several times. His mother held him close.

"Could I please just tell my story? Then I promise I'll give your sister back."

He buried his face in his mother's chest. "It will be okay," his mom reassured me. She patted Tommy's back and said, "Grandma told me there are toys behind that door. Let's go and play a while."

She carried the snuffling Tommy out through the door to the church hall.

Once again, I looked over the congregation. "Tommy loves his new sister. He'll be protecting her all her life," I said. "For just a few moments; he has reluctantly consented to let Diana be our baby Jesus. So let us begin again."

With that I stepped back into the spotlight, held baby Diana out to the congregation and began, "Just look at my Jesus. Isn't he beautiful..." The Spirit acted, and the magic of Christmas Eve descended.

*****

Reflection

Every time I think about Tommy and his claiming of his sister, I am reminded of our understanding of Jesus. Too often, we, too, want to claim him. "He's mine," we say. "My understanding, my way of worshipping, my faith is the only faith. He's not yours, he's mine. Attend my church, be a Christian just like me. That's the only way to God."

I believe God came in Jesus as a baby, not so we could own him, but so we could care for him. Babies seem fragile, helpless. They need us.

God needs us to care for the baby Jesus in every person we meet every day.

CAN I HOLD HIM?

SANTA? WHO, ME?

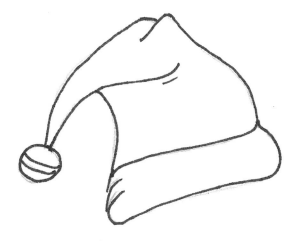

Introduction:

The few precious young people who are a part of our congregations tend to grow up and go away to college or university. Although they still come home for holidays. Too often, they seem to lose touch with the church. Sometimes, God acts to help them return. Although not a true story in my experience, something similar may have happened in yours.

SANTA? WHO ME?
I've Been to the Manger?

Christmas Eve day, I was having lunch with my parents. It was good to be home from university for the Christmas break. I had just offered to stay home and guard the house from thieves while they attended the late night Christmas Eve service at our church, when my cell phone rang.

"Merry Christmas," I said, into my phone, expecting one of my friends to return the greeting. Instead I heard the familiar voice of Rev. Margaret from our church.

"Merry Christmas to you, Richard. Welcome home. I'm so glad you had your phone turned on," Rev. Margaret said. "I serve on the hospital auxiliary, and we need someone to be Santa for the children's ward at the hospital tonight. Our regular Santa is sick. We don't want to disappoint the children. I remembered how you used to enjoy taking part in the plays when you were in Youth Group. Would you help us out, please?"

Me? Play Santa? I thought. *Now that's a joke.* Just last week, I had entertained my friends with a long rant on the whole Santa thing. In my mind, all Santa did was teach our already privileged children greed and selfishness. Besides, I wasn't bothering with church anymore.

Oh, I still believed in God. I hadn't forgotten everything. I just didn't need that church stuff, so why didn't I just say "No, thank you," and hang up? Well, even though I'm grown up, it's still hard to say no to Rev. Margaret. I like and respect her. Besides, how could I say no to a bunch of sick kids stuck in hospital on Christmas Eve.

I hesitated just long enough for Rev. Margaret to break the silence with, "Please Richard, you're really needed."

"All right," I said grudgingly.

I could hear the relief in her voice as she responded. "Thanks so much, Richard. Just think of this as fulfilling God's calling."

Yah right, I thought.

"I've the suit here at the church office. Could you come over now and get it?"

"Yah, sure." I responded. "See you in a few moments." I clicked off the phone and groaned as I shoved it into my pocket. When I vented my frustration with my parents, Mom grinned.

"You'll be fine," she said. "You're great with kids."

"Yah, right," I mumbled as I threw on my coat and headed to the church.

At six thirty, dressed in that scratchy Santa suit, and determined to get this ordeal over as quickly as possible, I stood listening to the muted babble of voices and laughter on the other side of the heavy doors of the children's ward. I clenched my teeth, pasted on a big smile and pushed on the doors.
"Ho, Ho, Ho…Merry Christmas," I hollered above the din.

"Santa," one of the little kids yelled.

Excited, pyjama-clad children swarmed around me, hugging my legs, reaching for my hands, pulling at my sack.

I winced inside. "Ho, Ho, Ho…slow down, children. There's enough for everyone," I said, while my brain registered, *See they're even greedy here at the hospital.*

Although the parents helped, it still took nearly an hour to speak with each child, answer their questions and give them their gift from the hospital auxiliary. I thought I was doing fine until the last child, Anthony, a boy about eight years old scoffed, "You're not Santa. You're too young."

A deafening silence fell. *How had they heard him in the midst of all this noise and confusion?* I wanted to say, *"You're right. This whole thing is ridiculous."* I looked at the littlest faces turned up at me, their lips quivering. My love for children and desire to please spoke for me. "Of course, I'm not Santa. I'm one of his helpers. Santa can't do it all alone, you know, especially tonight. He's got toys to deliver all over the world."

I could feel the relief come at me in waves as conversations, yelling and laughter started up again. Anthony, shook his head and walked slowly back to his room. Wanting desperately to give him reassurance of some kind, I followed. At the door of his room, Anthony turned around and looked up into my eyes. I could see his desperation.

"Okay, Santa's helper, if you're real, do your stuff," he spat at me.

Puzzled, I stepped into the dimly-lit room and watched Anthony, his spine stiff, march past his own bed, to a silent figure in the bed by the window.

"This is Grainger," he said. "Grainger's real sick and needs his mom. She's not here."

I looked down into Grainger's sad and frightened face. My stomach lurched. The whole issue of greed and Santa became irrelevant. A lump rose in my throat. Picking up Grainger's cold little hand, I thought, *What am I doing here? I can't fix this.* I was sure the kid could hear the frantic running of my brain, as I struggled to figure out what to say. As a last resort, I prayed, *"Help God. Rev. Margaret dragged me here. Help."*

The child's lifeless voice broke into my prayer. "Santa, how did you find me?"

I just opened my mouth and words spilled out. "Hi there, Buddy. You're in a tough spot. Did you think we'd all forgotten about you?"

Grainger nodded. A single tear slid down his cheek.

"Well, that's not true. There's Anthony here. He waited till I'd finished with all the kids out there, so he could bring me to you. You know what? I'm his Christmas gift to you from God. That's right. God loves you and has sent me here tonight because you needed me. God does that, you know."

Now, where did that come from? I thought. I took a deep breath. "What do you want for Christmas Grainger?" *Now, that's a totally insane question,* my brain nattered. *You've nothing to give this sick kid that he would want. Keep your mouth shut.*

Grainger's smile was weak and never made it to his eyes. "I …I…want…to be able to ride my bike again and play with my friends," he said, his voice muffled by the blankets.

Now what do I say to that? I don't even know what's wrong with this kid, I thought.

Young Anthony piped up, "Santa doesn't fix people, Grainger. He only brings gifts."

Thanks for rescuing me, I thought and reached into my pocket. I pulled out my new I-pod. "Fool," my brain shouted. "All you have on there is the classical stuff from your music history course." I handed the i-pod to Grainger. "You may not like the music on this," I said, "but someone around here will be able to load anything you want on it, games, music, whatever."

"Wow," both kids said in unison.

"Anthony's right, Grainger," I continued. "Santa doesn't fix people. Santa brings joy and laughter." My voice petered out. Silence surrounded us. I roused myself. "Guess, I'd better get going...Merry Christmas," I said and backed out of the room.

Whew! I'm glad that's over, I thought. As I turned toward the big double doors and freedom, I felt a light touch on my arm.

"Santa," a pretty young nurse said, "I realize you've been here a long time, but we've one more child that needs you. Please come this way."

Obediently, I followed her along the hospital corridor thinking, *maybe I can get a date with her*. We stopped at the door with a big red stop sign, and the words, "Quarantined."

"You'll have to gown up and wear a mask," she said. "This little one is infectious. I hope you don't mind."

Already overheated in false beard, wig and red velvet suit, I struggled into the gown, booties, gloves and mask.

"Her name is Alyssa," the nurse said. "She's five. Her parents had to go home to the rest of their children. She was asleep when they left. Now she's awake and afraid Santa won't find her tonight. Just talk to her for a moment, please."

I pushed open the door. "Ho, Ho Ho...Merry Christmas," I said, my voice as bright and happy as a hushed voice could manage.

Alyssa, sat up. A huge smile filled her face. "Santa, you're here. You found me," she sang out excitedly.

"Of course, I found you," I responded and reached down deep to the bottom of my nearly empty sack. There wasn't much left. My fingers touched a soft body. *This'll do*, I thought. *Whatever it is, she'll be able to cuddle it.* I pulled out a small, stuffed baby doll. Even its head was soft. Alyssa squealed with delight. "Here's someone to keep you company tonight," I said. "I'll leave the rest under the tree at your house. I'm sure your parents will bring your gifts here tomorrow."

"Thank you, Santa…Thank you…" Alyssa cradled the tiny doll in her arms. She looked up at me, her face serious. "My Mom said you wouldn't forget me, just because I'm in hospital. She said she asked God to make sure."

I grinned and thought, *this is the first time I've been an answer to prayer.* "I have to go now, Alyssa, I've a long journey tonight. You do as the doctors and nurses tell you." I patted her head. With my plastic glove I couldn't feel her black nappy hair, but I knew she could feel my touch.

"Merry Christmas, Santa," she said and lay back down her little body. She looked lost in the austere hospital bed.

"Merry Christmas," I answered. I picked up a bright pink blanket that had fallen on the floor and tucked it around her. "There now, you're ready for sleep. "

"MMMM," she said and cuddled down with her doll, her eyes heavy.

The revolving entrance door creaked as it spat me out into the cold winter evening. *I guess that wasn't so bad*, I thought..

On the way home, I drove past the church. Both sides of the road were lined with cars. Automatically, I slowed down and parked about a block away. Glancing at my watch, I hurried to the door, knowing the service had already started. As silently as possible, I slid through the big doors and stood at the back with several others. They looked at me with surprise. *Oh yes,* I thought, *I'm Santa Claus. Oh well, there's no reason why Santa can't come to church.*

Rev. Margaret was just finishing her message. "… Our Christmas story tells us that in Jesus, God came into the world needing our love. Every time we give and receive love, gifts and kindness, we figuratively kneel at the manger. May God Bless us all, tonight. Amen."

The opening chords of "Joy to the World" filled the church. I sang, my heart soaring, "Joy to the World, the Lord has come."

Tonight, I have been to the manger, I thought. *I brought joy to Jesus through the children. That's what I was doing at the hospital. Thank you God for asking me to be Santa.*

*****

CAN I HOLD HIM?

May you open your heart
this Christmas
and feel the blessing of the birth of Jesus
in your heart.

Merry Christmas!!

CAN I HOLD HIM?

Rev. Janet Stobie

Writer, storyteller, and ordained minister, Janet Stobie served nineteen years in parish ministry, retiring in 2009 to focus on her writing and her family. Janet particularly enjoys planning and conducting worship services. Her newspaper column *Today's Faith* and her blog *Tips for Grace-filled Living,* her short story collections, children's books and novel have been enthusiastically received. Janet's latest book, *Dipping Your Toes in Planning Small Group Devotionals*, is being used by lay leaders and clergy in United Churches across Canada. At present, she is writing a sequel to her novel *Fireweed.*

Sample & order Janet's books at
www.janetstobie.com

CAN I HOLD HIM?

Other Books Written by Janet Stobie

A Child Speaks
Biblically-based Short Stories

Spectacular Stella
Children's Picture Book

A Place Called Home
Homeless? Who, Me?

Fireweed
Mystery Novel & Grief Resource

Dipping Your Toes
In Planning Small Group Devotions
A Worship Resource

63307765R00093

Made in the USA
Charleston, SC
02 November 2016